A Jubilee Workbook

Defining And Planning Our Congregational Economic Development Mission

Karl C. Evans

CSS Publishing Company, Inc., Lima, Ohio

A JUBILEE WORKBOOK

For more information about CSS Publishing Company resources, visit our website at www.csspub.com or email us at csr@csspub.com or call (800) 241-4056.

ISBN-13: 978-0-7880-2608-9
ISBN-10: 0-7880-2608-9   PRINTED IN USA

This workbook is dedicated to ...

- *the congregations Donella and I have served across the nation. They have taught me as we worked together for the common good of the Lord's mission.*

- *the residents, workers, and congregations of the counties we have studied. Their joy and bitterness made economic development a personal issue in my ministry.*

- *the pastors of these counties, who have spilled their insides to me. Even the pastors who doubted that any good could come out of New York have helped. This includes a pastor who did not show up for a long-prearranged meeting for which I had traveled 1,000 miles.*

- *my parents, Margaret and Cecil Evans, who struggled to lift themselves, the family, and the community out of the grinding poverty of the Depression years.*

- *Doctor Doug Johnson of the General Board of Global Ministries of the United Methodist Church, who let me move on with the project.*

- *Donella, my wife, who has supported my work in so many ways.*

- *Dara, Kreg, Darcia, and D'arcy, our children, who have not allowed me the luxury of cheap statements.*

- *the Lord. Without the Lord, none of this would be reality.*

Table Of Contents

Foreword

Serving as pastor is a most difficult job. One very difficult portion of this work is defining, planning, and organizing for the mission of the congregation. As I have traveled and served around the United States I have tried to help as pastor after pastor struggled with their own ministry and that of their congregation.

This workbook is intended to help pastors in low-income communities sort out what they are to do. With poverty increasing in our world, economic development has to be one of our priorities. Very few organizations in the world have as much potential as the church of Jesus, the Christ, to impact economic development among low-income people of the world.

Perhaps this book will help guide this ministry.

— Karl Evans

A Church That Matters

A ringing phone after 10 p.m. in a pastor's home is trouble. That ring-a-ding-ding is a sure sign that someone needs help fast. It might be a frustrated parent, a frightened spouse, or a discouraged police officer. It could be anyone.

One time, though, the voice on my phone was that of a rural Mississippi pastor. We had met several months earlier. We came together for our common interests in the lowest-income rural counties in the US. Over pleasant glasses of iced tea we shared a few hours talking about his community. That Delta area was in the bottom ten rural counties in the nation for personal income.

Every caring pastor knows the critical value of personal income within the community. Financial income of the community is incredibly important to the well-being of the local church. The church lives on the contributions of its members and its non-member supporters. It can and should focus part of its mission work locally.

Some specific factors influence the economic life of the community. By working to comprehend the thinking of Jesus, the church will learn to search for new missions. It will find ways to support individuals, families, and communities in economic development.

Several months came and went. My report to the denomination was complete. That hard work rested securely and comfortably on a shelf in New York City, useless to anyone. The pastor and his congregation needed help immediately.

"What is the church prepared to do for us? We need help. Our people are starving. We pay in all that money for mission work. That is a part of being United Methodist. Then it goes to either New York or another foreign place. We are getting tired of that."

What he did not say rumbled through the conversation. He did not say the community was deciding whether to allow the support of a local casino gambling industry. He may have been primarily looking for some hope of stopping the gaming tables. The lure of casino industries is strong when the actual common unemployment rate runs above 70%.

When I told him the results of the study, he became terribly depressed and tearful. He mourned the money wasted for the study. I had to agree with him. But had we wasted the study money? I told him I would try to find out what I could. The pastor just hung up the phone without words of good-bye.

Since then I have spent much time revisiting and restudying these counties. My wife, Donella, and I have also visited many more counties with common needs. The counties in the original study were in a great circle of major poverty around the US. The states involved were Arizona, Utah, Colorado, New Mexico, Texas, Mississippi, Tennessee, Kentucky, South Dakota, North Dakota, and Montana.

We designed our project with the nation's lowest-income rural populations in mind. We knew most of these counties we visited held per capita incomes less than one-third that of the rest of the nation. Our purpose was to look for the result of the mission of the church. How could, should, and does this mission affect the economic well-being of the community? We assumed the whole body of Christ impacts the local church and community. Everywhere we looked, the denominations and sects, as unique organizations, have an enormous impact on the local area.

The sad songs of economic woe sounded repeatedly as I visited the other communities in the study. Often the songs voiced almost the same words. The phrases changed only with the variation in faith communities: United Methodist, Presbyterian, Roman Catholic, Mormon, and the like. Wherever there existed any ecclesiastic structure, I heard the same cry: "We send the money away willingly. That is the sort of Christians we try to be. We are among the lowest-income people of the world, and no money ever comes back. That hurts."

One overwhelming desire and need seems to fill these communities. A clear sense of hope abounds everywhere. Hundreds of people have agreed to the fact that financial stability for the local community begins at home. The root of economic development for the whole world is in local entrepreneurship. Newspapers and electronic media make headlines with the remote possibilities of major industries coming to town. However, this eventuality is more rare than top-grade caviar. If nothing else, we can and must be realistic in our approach. The issue then becomes the formation of guidelines by which the church may influence local entrepreneurship.

It is clearly true that many people dream of owning and operating businesses in their hometowns. They would love to go to the bank, borrow the money, purchase equipment, and make things happen. It is also clearly true that many expect to fail. In low-income areas, personal expectations of failure temper the drive to own and operate a business. This attitude pervades both the potential entrepreneurs and the community providers. It is corporate bloodletting. The bankers and the landlords and the politicians must support a project if it is to work. They must not expect to fail if their support is to be real. This rebuilt enthusiasm for local development is clearly a task for the church.

In most of these areas, adequate funding programs coming from state and federal sources and private programs exist. However, those who could and perhaps *should* establish business operations in the area just don't. It is in fostering entrepreneurship that the church and other nonprofit entities do their strongest work.

The church often falters in this area. Sometimes the church limits itself to overt evangelism or entertainment. Sometimes the church avoids talking about money or justice. In my research I have frequently heard that money and justice are not true concerns of the church. Salvation is the only concern, supposedly, for many.

The church has a history of fostering a distrust of local entrepreneurship. This distrust is most often as gossip, personal rivalries, and petty disputes. Even congregational or denominational competition can be negative in this area.

Often we can trace the distrust to inexperienced or uneducated clergy or lay workers. One successful farmer in the Rio Grande Valley of Texas left the United Methodist church terribly disappointed. He walked away after a staffer came down from New York City. He said, "That staffer told me that if I truly was successful, it was because I was cheating someone." This attitude soaked throughout the denomination at the time.

The church can and should look to our founder, our lord and master, Jesus of Nazareth. He was, among other things, quite an entrepreneur himself. The Messiah gathered and held together a small staff of non-experts. The Messiah changed the world with them. His finances were meager and his technology was limited. Yet, by his personal power he was successful in every way that finally mattered.

Jesus' great proof of his success is obvious. He changed lives. He changed every life on the planet. We need no additional proof.

As I have worked through this project, I have talked to hundreds of lay and professional people. Clergy, denominational leaders, economists, social scientists, and others have responded eagerly. Everyone I could find who would listen was interested. As I finished laying out the project and the learnings, almost all of them asked the same powerful question: "What is it you would have us do after we read the book and attend a workshop?" That is a fair question.

The answer is quite simple. As you read this material, you will become accustomed to thinking about the mission of Christ as your own. Economic development, entrepreneurship, and the mission of Christ will come to a common focus for your community. You will enhance your own ability to focus the mission of your faith group or other nonprofit entity on life itself. You will own the economic development and entrepreneurship needs of your community as a right mission of your faith. This study is an attempt to help make these needs plain and define specific processes to fill those needs.

You will choose your own programs, goals, tactics, and strategies. These should align with the needs of your own members and the rest of the community. If the community needs self-esteem, for instance, you will program your mission in that direction. Your own efforts and the efforts of others will back the mission of Christ.

I have great trust in the good-faith action of the working people. If folks can respond to their faith with God by doing good, they will. If their response is in doing good toward their fellow human beings, I believe they will do just that. They just need to understand how. That is the point of the project and this workbook.

Getting Started
In Our Own Community

A fountain of resources exists within the church for economic development. In small rural areas it often lies stagnant. Most of this fountain is willingly untouched. Many Christians have tried to tell me that economic development is not a concern of the church. Pastors sometimes seem to allow the financial needs of their members to go unsupported by the congregation and pastor. They sometimes claim the church is for theological matters such as a rescue from hell. Some say we might even toss in teaching prayer and theology. Perhaps we may use the church to get us ready for an eternity in heaven.

This statement of irrelevance comes also from many who avoid the church in low-income communities. Many of these people agree with the useless and irrelevant nature of the church. Money talks. Yet, if the church does not talk about money, it is not part of the mission of Christ.

The issues of community support seem not to be of any major interest right now. If this is so, they can safely ignore the church. A lifelong Roman Catholic in Antonito, Colorado, was very frustrated with the church. "I want to hear the priest talking and making sense about the things that are important to me today. When he does, I will be in Mass every day. Most of what the pope says doesn't interest me at all. It does not affect me or my life."

Economic development support is a wide-open field for the mission of Christ. The church and other charitable nonprofits in the US are quite capable. Around the world, we have the tools and the personnel to step in and make a huge difference. People plainly want support from Christ in their daily lives. This support comes first and best from local congregations.

So the question becomes, how do folks spend their daily lives? It's an easy answer. People in North America spend most of their lives trying to make a living. We choose not just survival but getting comfortable financially. For most of the world, gathering money is critically important to individuals, families, and communities. The church ignores this matter at its own peril.

In any community, the church must live out its mission. It must accept as its mission certain factors that are the clear responsibility of the faith community. No one else will offer them. If the people are to enjoy the ability to gather money, the faith community must do its share. Without these factors, the community will not make progress in its economic, social, psychological, and spiritual levels. Where any of these factors are missing, the community effort to cycle money falters in some way. These missing factors have led to the writing of this evaluation tool. I have used nearly forty years of professional pastoral, teaching, and research ministry to build this tool.

Listening and learning about people in poverty across our nation has shaped my understanding. A drastic shortage of money rocks their whole lives. My parents married and started a family during the depths of the Great Depression. They moved to an area newly supplied with irrigation water. The neighbors bought or homesteaded land during very difficult times. Of those who tried in that community, 90% eventually gave up. My service and study have now taken me into about 150 of the lowest per capita income counties of the US.

Many nonprofit fraternal and service groups of every kind beyond the church found their responsibilities. Although I looked for work specific to the church, I found it easy to translate this work to any nonprofit group. Every group has its own mission. Elks, the Masonic Orders, Veterans of Foreign Wars, 4-H clubs, Odd Fellows, Grange, hospital auxiliaries, and more have developed their own chosen tasks. Every group has its own words, structures, and styles to substitute into the study outcome.

The possible economic development mission of the church is also easy to picture as the mission of your own family. Almost every family hopes everyone in the family will gain the ability to be financially comfortable at some level. The work of economic development for family is not just a matter of earning a few more dollars each day. Personal economic development is a matter of preparing your own family to better itself economically.

Now, as we look at our own hometowns we can find a variety of factors that affect economic lives. Each of these is important. Each of these is open to influence from many different sides.

Spreading this list of income factors around the community can be very helpful. Many have not considered the factors needed for community economic growth. They include the kind of work reserved for governments, banks, major industries, or public relations firms. These "for profit" firms and government entities hold specific tasks. They can and should work in most of the areas listed in this document. Every successful private industry and governmental office takes the work seriously. It is a standard function of success. However, major responsibilities continue in these areas for the church and other nonprofit groups, including families.

At the close of the formal study of these lowest-income counties, I began to visit more areas. My intent has been to redevelop and refine a major list of factors. These would, and should, be mission targets for local congregations and larger church entities.

Donella and I have talked with people across the US and Canada. Our RV has been through some of the weakest areas of the nation. We have listened, groped for words, and asked countless questions. We have shared ideas, cried, and laughed as the humanity of these areas has revealed itself to us.

After all this, we have come to a deeper respect for the insights of the people we have met. Pastors, homeless, entrepreneurs, children, educators, and more.

In this light, perhaps the most fascinating group we found was in Tunica, Mississippi. FCCCOT (Former Concerned and Concerned Citizens of Tunica) has an impact. Members of this group have spent at least part of their lives in Tunica County. Many have moved away from Tunica. In their hearts, they continue to feel that Tunica County, and particularly the Tunica school system, need their support. They contribute money, leadership, prayers, and dream development to the community, whether they live in Tunica or in Detroit.

This study series consists largely of responses to a tool we found helpful and easy to use. While we have tried to help, we have first tried to comprehend. This tool has been a labor of love

15

and inquiry. Many churches and other groups have used it to help develop their own mission to their communities.

We invite you to gather some of your congregation or non-profit group together. Such a group will enable a broad evaluation of realities and introduction to the possibilities of the future. Fraternal groups, service clubs, educational fellowships, and many other gatherings can adapt this tool. The most significant factor lies in identifying the group's own mission. For many, the real mission in the community exists in developing entrepreneurship and economic growth.

You probably will choose to score your own community and congregation. At some point you may wish to apply the scale to your entire culture. My study of the church in support of economic development has covered several distinct cultures. These cultures create a great circle of American poverty.

First, the Four Corners area of New Mexico, Arizona, Utah, and Colorado. The Navajo nation dominates the Native American nations here. Hopi, Zuni, and many others make up a broad spectrum of life. Some issues are common among these peoples. Other issues vary widely among the groups.

Second, the northern plains people. Again, the lower-income peoples are primarily Native American. The Sioux are predominant. Much of this community centers around South Dakota, especially Pine Ridge. Many nations live within 500 miles of Pine Ridge. Wounded Knee is the icon for this portion.

Third, the southern Appalachian area. This population is primarily Anglo and centered around Hazard, Kentucky. It includes areas within about 200 miles of Hazard in several states. Major industries include coal, tobacco, and timber.

Fourth, the Mississippi Delta includes both sides of the Mississippi River country, from Cairo, Illinois, to the Gulf of Mexico. Large sections of this area are almost entirely a black population. Many former residents have moved to northern industrial centers along the rust belt. Now they are returning as the rust belt employment weakens.

Fifth, the Rio Grande Valley, from Brownsville, Texas, to Alamosa, Colorado. This long area is a true border community in every sense of the word. The Rio Grande River border with Mexico reaches only along the river as far as El Paso. The Anglo-Latin community extends to Alamosa. Many families cover the entire length of the Rio Grande. People move along both sides of the river regularly. They migrate, visit, study, and otherwise develop their lives as citizens of a lengthy community. It may well be the most cosmopolitan area of the US outside New York City.

On a personal note, I have developed this study and program guide primarily from my own experiences. Therefore, much of the material is from my own life. As you read this, please forgive the frequent first-person pronouns.

My own early development has helped me comprehend the role of the church in economic development. In 1939, the only sign of the coming Nu Acres community was the promise of irrigation water coming to the area between Fruitland and Caldwell, Idaho. This area, about 2,000 square miles, was to be irrigated by water from the Black Canyon dam and reservoir at Emmett.

Few people lived in the area in 1939. Probably fewer than a thousand people inhabited the entire area, living off sheep and cattle ranching, and the promise of brighter days to come.

My parents bought forty acres in a particularly good area. Through the winter of 1939-40, they worked to build a rudimentary house. The family moved to the area in February 1940. I arrived in April.

Our task those first few years was overwhelming. We built our house. We developed the farm. We brought together marketing systems and fire protection. We developed an entire community, complete with a Grange, a ladies' club, a store, schools, roads, street signs, and everything else needed for a rural community.

We had help, of course, and we helped each other. Especially in light of this project, we had the churches. I can clearly recall times of great help as we worked for our community.

At church, we learned many secrets of community development. We studied the Ten Commandments and the Beatitudes. We read about the life of Christ and the writings of Paul. We studied how King Saul and David worked to develop Israel.

Our pastors often talked about some of these matters in their sermons. Or we practiced some community development rituals in the church gatherings.

Then we went home. When we went home, we spread those concepts around the community and our family. Often I was amazed by the direct ways the words and systems of the pastor and congregation found their way into our family and community life!

The Reverend Doctor Enoch Nye was one of the best. This quiet, reserved, careful man made a great impact on our lives through his sermons and congregation development.

In any case, he knew the secret to lasting impact on our little community. Lead people to Christ, and teach them the ways of the Lord.

Go into your own house and community, my friends, and do likewise.

Defining A Mission Of Economic Development For Christian Congregations And Other Nonprofits

As you work through this study tool, the questions will be simple and heart-wrenching. The words are easy. The choices you must make will force difficult decisions.

In your community and church, what is your evaluation of each of these areas of life? You, as pastor, officer, citizen, teacher, deacon, elder, student, or member, have the responsibility. You have no leeway to raise the issue of personal poverty without personally taking stock of potential cures. We also need to remember that God never asks us to take any action without God's involvement.

The New Testament literature portrays Jesus as working with extremely low-income people and also with the wealthy. His work was not limited to healing physical problems. Social issues, emotional patterns, and economic realities made up much of his work. Jesus did not just make the blind see, or the deaf hear, or cleanse the lepers. He also worked with the wealthy, the healthy, the politically powerful, and the middle classes.

Jesus impressed many with their responsibility for the world. "You are the salt of the earth." "This woman who has given a coin has given much." "Turn away from your family and neighbors to make the world righteous."

Under the title of each section of this little study guide are three blank spaces. You and your congregation may use these spaces to help you estimate and understand your own needs and mission. The congregation must take ownership of these numbers. In these matters, the pastor's opinion has no more weight than that of anyone else. The primary task of the pastor is to pull these matters out of the congregation.

Use a scale of zero to ten (0-10), with ten being high. In the first space, give your community a mark for the general level of

19

the factor. Take into account all you know about your community, its history, and its people. Be as critical and as complete as you wish. No one will call you wrong for your judgment. It is very personal.

Then in the second space, give your congregation a reality mark for itself. Again, lift up as much as you wish about your congregation and your denomination. Consider your administration, the gatherings, mission programs and giving, worship, sacramental style, and others. Ask: Does the congregation know and represent the community?

In the third space, use the same scale. Estimate the strength and will of the congregation to commit itself to build healthy factors in your community. Ask yourself what Jesus would say or do when faced with the needs of the people in your community today. These needs will be the same for all people, whether in the US or other nations. Perhaps we should ask what Jesus did, according to the gospels. Then we could judge our own efforts accordingly.

I have tried to sharply limit my generalizations. Be as specific as possible as you work on these questions for yourself and your community. Check your perceptions by getting opinions and feelings from a broad spectrum of your community. Especially, check with those who seem to have some overt desire to move ahead economically. Ask them to be very honest in their assessment of the community realities.

Be extremely honest. You are not doing this exercise to make yourself or someone else feel good. You are doing it to fit better into the way the creator works.

Make many notes. We never know when a random thought will change us. It may give us serendipitous insight into our own lives or the lives of others. Brainstorms, ideas, and notions should fill your study pages. Jot down everything you hear. It may prove important later.

This discussion will always be incomplete. Every person who studies this material should be comfortable adding repeatedly to the list of issues and consequences. The same structure can and should be effective for any other potential or current effect of ministry.

Always look to your source of knowledge and understanding for help. The *Wesleyan Quadrilateral* is a common evaluation tool of sources of understanding and hope. Scripture, history, reason, and personal experience provide the base under this scheme.

This series should give your congregation a few handles for fulfilling the needs of the community. Some of it may seem to be overlapping. Other parts may even seem contradictory. You will probably find a factor or two to add to this list. I do not claim to have found every issue. Nevertheless, when you struggle with each factor, you will find help as you develop the ministry of your congregation.

Fifteen separate areas rise for evaluation. Be certain to record the scores you give each area of study. As your community congregations and other groups prepare their mission work, they will want to know these scores. If you are honest in your preparation, your priorities for mission will be based on these scores.

The Reality Of Community

> *"I am the true vine, and my Father is the vinegrower.
> He removes every branch in me that bears no fruit.
> Every branch that bears fruit he prunes to make it bear
> more fruit. You have already been cleansed by the words
> that I have spoken to you. Abide in me as I abide in
> you. Just as the branch cannot bear fruit by itself unless
> it abides in the vine, neither can you unless you abide
> in me. I am the vine, you are the branches ... This is my
> commandment, that you love one another as I have loved
> you. No one has greater love than this, to lay down
> one's life for one s friends...."* — John 15:1-5a, 12-13

For humans, the sense of community is perhaps most difficult
to comprehend. We have a seemingly normal tendency to understand human relationships in dramatically objective and first-person singular terms. Our current advertisements on television focus
on our needs. Our present sermons seem to focus on our responsibilities and our relationship with Christ. Even our searches for mari-
tal partners focus on our desires, our hopes, and our dreams.

We talk in very objective ways about percentages of marriages
that survive or fail. We note that some percentage of the population attends church. Panic sets in when we find that we have some
number of our population in prison. These numbers are interesting
and even sometimes helpful. On the other hand, they entirely miss
the point of personal community.

In God's world, community includes three people or groups of
people.

Imagine a three-sided conversation, a relationship such as is
common in human life. Imagine a girl who cannot choose between
two boys. Think of the relationship between a father, a mother, and

23

a newborn child. Consider the relationship of a judge, a prosecutor, and the accused. For the faith community, the three people in the relationship are God, you, and me.

Several principles are at work in our three-sided relationship. First, the little community includes everyone and everything affected by the actions and thoughts of any other. No one and no thing can be cut out of our community based on a notion. These relationships include the men and women who are in prison. They include the soldiers and leaders of the nations with whom we have been at war. They include people who have never attended church and perhaps never will.

Second, the relationships portrayed here show the give and take relationships in every direction among the three. Each of these lines is the direct responsibility of the two parties on the ends of that line. This is easy to see. My relationship with God is God's responsibility, and it is my responsibility.

This relationship is also a responsibility of the third party of the community as well. It is the responsibility of the "other" in the triangle. Sometimes the "other" can make direct impact on this God-Me relationship by affecting my life somehow. Sometimes the "other" can speak to God directly, perhaps for me.

This is true all around the community, the faith community as we know it. God has some, but not all, responsibility for my relationship with other humans. It is a clear statement of most faith groups that God does affect our human relationships with each other. God acts in unlimited ways for us. Moreover, we have an evangelical mission for each of us. We are to take responsibility for the relationship between God and our neighbor. This is the radical side of the Shema backed up by the golden rule.

This understanding of community is core to the effectiveness of this discussion. Whether or not you have economic health is a concern and a responsibility to me and to our Lord. We have the obligation to make your relationships better if we can understand how. This is the mission of Christ, and it is the mission of the church. Whether we consider ourselves Christian, Hindu, Muslim, or whatever is almost irrelevant.

All of us must face part of this issue. We must choose whether we operate within this universe in a way that fits with the creator's vision. Vision is not only an issue of whether we believe the Judeo-Christian God is boss. It is also an issue of inclusiveness. Will we commit ourselves to fit properly into all the systems envisioned by our creator?

Jesus came among us to make human life as good as possible. He did not attempt to handle the entire task by himself. He chose to open creation to us with his life. Christ has shown us what we need, removed the only barrier to perfection, and invited us to get on board. He simplified the discussion dramatically. He eliminated the guilt barrier between the creator and us. Jesus personally voided any price of sin for us.

Because Jesus makes our own lives that good, our response will include taking that mission on toward each other. Any relationship reflects in some way every other relationship in one's life. My relationship with you varies with my relationship with Christ. My relationship with Christ shouts something of my relationship with you.

A very common question heard in Christian classes opens the door to our task. The question is simple: "Why did Jesus live and die and come out of the tomb?"

The answer is a simple one: "Jesus came to make human life the best possible." Our task in economic development is precisely that — to do everything possible to make human life as good as it can be, regardless of the risk. That task includes economic development.

Factor 1
The Sense Of Creation

Community Reality =   _____
Congregational Reality =   _____
Congregational Mission =   _____

> *O Lord, our Sovereign, how majestic is your name in all the earth!*
>
> *You have set your glory above the heavens. Out of the mouths of babes and infants you have founded a bulwark because of your foes, to silence the enemy and the avenger.*
>
> *When I look at your heavens, the work of your fingers, the moon and the stars that you have established; what are human beings that you are mindful of them, mortals that you care for them?*
>
> *Yet you have made them a little lower than God, and crowned them with glory and honor. You have given them dominion over the works of your hands; you have put all things under their feet, all sheep and oxen, and also the beasts of the field, the birds of the air, and the fish of the sea, whatever passes along the paths of the seas.*
>
> *O Lord, our Sovereign, how majestic is your name in all the earth!* — Psalm 8

Statement Of Reality

Individuals, families, and organizations can function with God's creative activity recognizable in their words, actions, and relationships. When someone looks at the life of the community, the best response is clear: We are genuinely thankful that God has set us down in this place and time, as a gift.

What are the people of your community and congregation that God is mindful of them?

As you read Psalm 8, hear the words and their flow as coming from your creator. God creates you as a person-being because God wants to love you.

What is there in this passage that speaks to your inner self? Read several translations of this passage to gain a deeper understanding of the sense of the passage. You might list a half dozen issues of your deepest consciousness. Then consider how this passage speaks to each of these issues.

How are these words passed to you in any way through history? To say it another way, why do you have these words about the thinking of God? You might trace the path of this transmission from creation to today. Just trace them from the ancient Hebrews living in what is now Iraq to yourself. What is there about living where and when you are that affects how this passage touches you? Use all the space and time you need to trace these patterns between God and you from then until now.

What impact do these emotions of God have on your sense of who you are? Remember that everyone's feelings are as valid and important as anyone else's feelings. While your actions are not as powerful as God's actions at times, your feelings are just as important. God did not say that Adam and Eve should not feel as they did. They were just not to take some specific actions that did not fit the vision of God for the world.

A strong sense of community implies a good sense of creation. Reality includes a sense of community as a personal gift from God. This gift is for the benefit of humankind. It therefore merits as much respect, gratitude, concern, and understanding as can be mustered. God creates the world and humankind, then comes to us bearing the additional gifts of the Spirit and the Christ. As a response to the creator, the whole community has intense concern for matters of ecology and resources.

Within the Hopi nation of Arizona exists a powerful sense of the creator. Rituals of dance, song, and meditation are more than art forms. They typically focus our senses on living within the dreams of the creator. From the high mesas of the reservation, the

Hopi can and do survey the world around them from now until tomorrow. Surveying this world spiritually provides a set of unique possibilities. The people accept for themselves some responsibility. Possibilities and careful action are called for by the creator's vision. The vision exists openly within the creator's dream for the world. Those with spiritual senses will know this mission.

The Bible tells of the Hebrews struggling with the understanding of themselves in creation. They knew their call was not to destroy the earth, to use it up. God wanted them to share the further creative activity with God's own self. They knew the importance of mimicking God's intent and action in the creation. God ejected Adam and Eve from Eden when they chose to operate apart from God's intentions. Walking hand-in-hand with God is a requirement.

The Bible speaks often of humankind's role in creation. We are both created and co-creator. We are to name the animals, to civilize the universe, and to spread peace and justice everywhere. Our attempts to do this are marks of faithfulness. Our unwillingness to do this work in concert with our loving God is a matter for forgiveness and redemption.

Questions For Evaluation

- Does our community understand itself as sharing God's creative work?
- Does the church lead the community in learning the possibilities of the creative process?
- Is the church able to say that responsible entrepreneurship is a legitimate part of sacred creation labor?

Examples

Following a lectionary of some sort will nearly always find us using at least one of the biblical creation stories in worship during the year. Often this celebration comes at the first of the calendar year, but not necessarily.

At some time through the year the congregation will vividly recall the creation in whatever way it chooses. Usually this will coincide with lectionary processes. We can study several creation stories found in Judeo-Christian and other scriptures. Some of these can readily be presented in poetry, music, technical drama, art, and so on. The style is open to creativity.

* * *

Sometime between 600 BC and 480 BC, the Hebrews were in captivity in Babylon. They were slaves, doing the will of the Babylonians. The real struggle, though, was remembering their own creation story and rejecting the Babylonian creation stories. In the church, we occasionally serve well if we spend a little time retelling both stories. Then we can understand our own a little better. Good texts for this material exist in many local and regional libraries. A well-recognized form of the old Babylonian/Akkadian story is the *Enuma Elish*. We translate this title best with: "When on high...."

Middle school and senior high students especially enjoy presenting the *Enuma Elish*. Using Ezekiel as a base helps this study. The comparison of biblical and Akkadian stories provides exciting dramatic readings and plays.

* * *

Many possibilities exist for ecological emphasis during the year. We can study, celebrate, pray, sing, or simply read from the vast supply of ecology material that exists today. We can find special speakers or pull together groups for many different emphases. Simple acts of restoration are effective. Cleaning up some portion of the environment or celebrating birds singing can add to the understanding and sense of creation.

* * *

Almost every community has an annual celebration of some sort. The church has the option of taking a leadership role in these. The church can move the festivities into a celebration of the gift of life and creation itself. It can do this without becoming obnoxiously evangelistic.

*   *   *

Freedom of religious expression and theology includes the right to live within one's own understanding of the creator's dream. Using such passages as the psalms is an easy way to hold a great variety of self-understanding in liturgy.

Brainstorm

What are your own creative thoughts for building the sense of creation?

1. What evidence have you found to support the rating you have given your own community?

2. What evidence have you found to support the rating you have given your congregation?

3. What biblical passages do you find relevant to these needs and concepts?

4. What programs might work in your church and community?

5. What will your work be in this process?

6. How will you reveal these thoughts to your church and community?

Notes

Factor 2
Vision In Community

Community Reality = _____
Congregational Reality = _____
Congregational Mission = _____

> *Then I saw a new heaven and a new earth; for the first
> heaven and the first earth had passed away, and the
> sea was no more. And I saw the holy city, the new
> Jerusalem, coming down out of heaven from God,
> prepared as a bride adorned for her husband. And I
> heard a loud voice from the throne saying, "See, the
> home of God is among mortals ... he will wipe every
> tear from their eyes. Death will be no more; mourning
> and crying and pain will be no more, for the first things
> have passed away." And the one who was seated on
> the throne said, "See, I am making all things new."*
> — Revelation 21:1-3a, 4-5a

Statement Of Reality

The individuals and organizations of the community are keenly
aware of their situation. They have adopted a very detailed view of
the future of their community. The people see in this scenario the
best possible life for themselves and the people around them. The
people see this as the first gift of the creator to the community.

Christ has shared with us the divine vision for our world and
for the life to come. He has told us what God wants and expects
and works to make real. It is also what God knows to be in our best
interest.

It is the nature of God to do whatever is in our best interest. Dr.
Max Miller, one of my seminary instructors and a great thinker

and scholar, had a key statement here. When Moses asked God, "Whom shall I say is sending me?" God answered, "Yahweh."

Dr. Miller says the best translation of the word "Yahweh" is the most emotionally packed: "At the risk of my own existence, I will do whatever I can to make your existence as good as possible." This divine vision is lived out in Jesus. In his mission, Jesus risks everything for the good of humans. If Jesus had not come out of the tomb, the creation would have collapsed. Since Jesus did come out of the tomb, life for humans gets better and better.

The book of Revelation is forward-looking nostalgia. The Reverend Eddie Fox of the United Methodist Church General Board of Discipleship calls it "Aiglatson." He says it is "nostalgia" spelled backward and looking forward. Because we look forward to it, we find ourselves drawn to help make it happen. It is not just busy work for the disciples. It is even more than an invitation to share in the kingdom of the Lord. Just as are the parables of the kingdom, this vision is active. The parables build us into the kingdom in some sense, whether or not we decide to enter it.

Part of this vision, as clearly seen in the gospels, is good, responsible, ethical, successful business. That is good for everyone. Jesus does not reject business. He calls it to reflect God's vision of the world. It seems that the vision assumes that profitable business is at least acceptable, perhaps even encouraged directly.

Of course, this does not mean that financial profit is the only end of business. It says that the kingdom and its vision path can include financial profit.

The book of Revelation takes the Sermon on the Mount and applies it to the future: "And I saw another world, a world not made with hands." Obviously, God will be a willing participant in our creative efforts. Our Savior's relationship with us will shape our relationships with each other.

If we live by the Sermon on the Mount, what sort of world will we have? The Beatitudes are the new Ten Commandments. These are a promise of the future. They are also a call to sacred righteousness and effective faithfulness in our dealings with each other. Most specifically, "Blessed are those who hunger and thirst after righteousness, for they shall be filled."

34

The Beatitudes make a powerful ethics statement for a major or minor business operation or chamber of commerce mission statement. Yet the world's businesses often attempt to compete with everything short of death to the loser.

The Lord's vision for the world, shared with us, is the primary theme of the book of Revelation. Revelation 7:16 ff says, "They will hunger no more, and thirst no more; the sun will not strike them, nor any scorching heat .. and God will wipe away every tear from their eyes."

The importance of the gospel to the world is made clear in the Sermon on the Mount. Living that way would be the result of walking with God as if back in the Garden. The new world would be the paradise on earth that Adam and Eve abandoned. They chose not to share creation labor with God. Economic well-being in the community is possible. It will require adopting the vision of God that we know from Jesus.

The community outwardly and inwardly shares the vision. Our community promotes that vision among newcomers and succeeding generations. Values that will lead to the fulfillment of that vision live in the hearts and minds of the community. We teach them to each other. We live them out in our relationships.

Questions For Evaluation
- Does our community have a common vision for its own future and the future of the world?
- If so, is this vision built on sacred perspectives?
- Does the church constantly study the community vision for areas that need restructuring and revision?
- Does the church practice the vision of the community and God?

Examples
Sacred vision is the same as sense of creation, but pointed in the opposite direction. We look to Genesis for guidance on creation. We look to Revelation for guidance on the sacred vision. The church could and probably should include statements from the vision in every service.

The book of Revelation makes beautiful fodder for poetry, drama, and music. "Aiglatson" is an easy subject for liturgies for the local congregation. The traditional forms and elements of vision work well when given a contemporary or futurist twist.

* * *

The church at prayer can regularly speak to God about the vision of the future. Every prayer that includes an element of confession should contain an element of redemption and vision. Our understanding of our relationship with God is to be a contact with past and future. The vision of our creator includes the notion that our past does not necessarily determine our future. We can change, especially if we move in the direction of fitting more closely into our creator's vision.

* * *

The church can and should actively participate in community planning and election processes. An active congregation might invite various speakers to come explain their sense of vision for the community. The congregation might make registration to vote a normal part of church membership. Without some actions of this nature, the church is entirely otherworldly. This would not be in the call from Christ. The sacred vision is not just unrealistic thinking. It is a call to action by faithful people.

* * *

The church might develop its own vision for the community, then present it to the planning board and the rest of the community for discussion and action. Christ calls his church to lead the world and also to follow him.

* * *

The church might develop its vision for the community, then prepare various plans of action aimed at making this vision come true. This might include very specific details, especially including actions for which the congregation must and can take responsibility.

*   *   *

One outstanding sacred vision power operates in the sand paintings of Navajo sacred people. If a person is ill, the patient or others in the family may call the sacred person to attend. That person heals by the ritual of sand painting. At the appointed time, the sacred person begins the work. The ill person is present, if possible, with the family and close friends around.

The healer pours sand of various colors on the ground. The healer is free to follow whatever design comes to the hand. While the healer works, the healer tells a story or relates a vision. The work may take a few hours or a few days. At a very precise moment the sand painting is announced as satisfactory to the creator and thus complete. The healing is fulfilled.

Then the witnesses celebrate, pay the healer, and go home. Physicians and other healers have long known of the powers of prayer and vision. Most of us also have a keen awareness of the opposition of prayer and vision against self-destruction and despair.

Brainstorm

What are your own creative thoughts that may help build the community vision?

1. What evidence have you found to support the rating you have given your own community?

2. What evidence have you found to support the rating you have given your congregation?

3. What biblical passages do you find relevant to these needs and concepts?

4. What programs might work in your church and community?

5. What will be your work in this process?

6. How will you reveal these thoughts to your church and community?

Notes

Factor 3
Capability In Community

Community Reality = _____
Congregational Reality = _____
Congregational Mission = _____

> *But Moses said to the Lord, "O my Lord, I have never been eloquent, neither in the past nor even now that you have spoken to your servant; but I am slow of speech and slow of tongue."*
>
> *Then the Lord said to him, "Who gives speech to mortals? Who makes them mute or deaf, seeing or blind? Is it not I, the Lord? Now go, and I will be with your mouth and teach you what you are to speak."*
>
> — Exodus 4:10-12

Statement Of Reality

The community people have developed the skills, knowledge, resources, and personal qualities to renew themselves and reinvent their future. They learn collectively and individually. Learning, itself, has a high priority as a community activity.

Since the beginning of civilization, education has been an active mission of successful communities. Teachers at all levels and in all environments have spoken of their occasional confusion of missions. Sometimes book learning seems nothing more than driving data into the brain, just as filling a tub with water. At other times, rote learning becomes an end. Perhaps the wildest failure is in religious education. Here, it is God's own vision, purpose, and tools that are at stake. Teachers who see themselves in partnership with the Lord may take their own calling more seriously.

Teachers, administrators, and support personnel tend to become more excited when education is much more than rote learning. It is that tool that opens people to new options of life, especially the options arranged by their creator. With a little knowledge, the people can rearrange their lives. They become more able to live according to Christ's vision.

The Sunday school movement began as an attempt by the church to bring literacy to the masses of the world. Today's Protestantism uses education largely as an evangelistic tool. This is sad, for education has the potential to be so much more. Church education could bring ethics, logic, geography, morality, art, and many more subjects as gifts to the people. This, in turn, creates in the students and community a much more capable society.

Religious education has often succumbed to parental temptation. It can become a time-killer or babysitting tool for the local congregation. Teachers give students platitudes and moralistic recruiting homilies and nonsense recreation. Christ calls for faith-building work that opens tomorrow as we work through today.

As a pastor who has tried to be faithful, I have sometimes struggled. I have tried to answer one question at the close of every worship service, class, board or committee meeting: "What have I learned here, and what have others learned?" The answer to this can be stimulating and frustrating.

Questions For Evaluation
- Does our community and our church share an active commitment to skills education for everyone as a means toward a better life?
- Does the church always function as an educational organization?

Examples
The church might lift up the various community teachers in celebration. Gather the group together and reinforce their commitment with praise, songs, pictures, meals, and whatever else it may take. The group should include workers from many different arenas. Public schools, religious schools, charter schools, private

schools, home schools, Sunday schools, immigrant education, colleges and universities, senior hostels, hospital dietitians, and any others that exist in your community. Celebrate them and point out their value in God's vision.

*   *   *

The church can host classes and tutoring programs in any area it wishes. Providing facilities, leadership, and administration for literacy classes is easy and appropriate. It is a mission action as easy as reading the Sermon on the Mount. For those who choose to pursue the vision of Christ, it is appropriate. In 1976-1977, the schools of Cottage Grove, Oregon, were closed for lack of funding. Teachers from the schools voluntarily met their classes in various churches and other buildings in town.

*   *   *

In the worship service itself, the congregation learns literacy and language in many simple ways. Extremely young children can learn to pray using pictures in a special bulletin along with words.

*   *   *

The church might officially or individually involve themselves with the various surveys of the schools in the area taken each year. It can look at the results of test scores, college success rates, and other tools. The church can be involved.

*   *   *

In selecting leaders, a most worrisome thing is the tendency of congregations to choose their most experienced and trained people. This may be a dreadful error for several reasons.

First, many of us would like to spread our abilities into larger areas of life. Many accountants, for instance, rebel at being limited to the treasurer's role.

Second, most of us enjoy learning new work and taking on new responsibilities. I have often wished to quarterback a football team. I will never have that opportunity.

Third, spreading the training around forces an inclusiveness that just won't come any other way.

Given these ideas, perhaps the congregation could commit itself to a three-year term in an area. The congregation can and should set its own limits. One year for training, a second year as chair, and a third year serving the area.

If the training is strong, we know many in our congregations who can and will do the work. We may give up the question "Who can do the work right now?" and ask "Who can we train to do the work?" People who want to learn to operate a business can learn to handle financial matters. Those who intend to pursue a teaching career can look at issues of the church school.

As a junior high school football coach, one of our league rules was a matter of inclusiveness. Every player was to play in every game. I will never forget the look on one young man's face when I forgot to get him into a game. It broke my heart and his.

Brainstorm

What are your own creative thoughts to help the community become more capable?

1. What evidence have you found to support the rating you have given your own community?

2. What evidence have you found to support the rating you have given your congregation?

3. What biblical passages do you find relevant to these needs and concepts?

4. What programs might work in your church and community?

5. What will be your work in this process?

6. How will you reveal these thoughts to your church and community?

Notes

Factor 4
Commitment In Community

Community Reality =   _____
Congregational Reality =   _____
Congregational Mission =   _____

> *"Whoever comes to me and does not hate father and mother, wife and children, brothers and sisters, yes, and even life itself, cannot be my disciple. Whoever does not carry the cross and follow me cannot be my disciple."* — Luke 14:26-27

Statement Of Reality

People are an active part of the experience of creating something together. There are existing common commitments to the vision. Strong processes live that enable folks to develop commitments to each other and to the value structure. The church has an active leadership role in developing these commitments.

When the Hebrews under Joshua were ready to come out of the wilderness, they knew their task would be difficult. Some who thought they could simply cross the Jordan River and set up the new nation were disappointed. Most knew the task would be horrendous and very costly.

The Hebrews were committed, however. They embarked on the struggle and were eventually successful building the nation. The task took many years, with confusing ups and downs, but they kept their commitment. Their commitment was not just a self-serving platitude but a statement of faith as well.

This commitment to the Lord was the major human effort toward success. The commitment of the community has been and still is a major task while doing economic development. From

Genesis to Revelation, every writer has emphasized commitment as part of the faith relationship.

Questions For Evaluation
- Do we know ourselves as committed to our community and our common vision?
- Is everyone included in the processes that strengthen our commitment?
- How do we justify asking ourselves and our neighbors for commitment?

Examples
For commitment to build, we must develop certain patterns. Ownership by the masses in the community is essential. A vision that exists only in the minds and hearts of a few is a vision that will likely fail. The church can spread the word and build the commitment, even in communities with no other media. Telephone campaigns, meetings, and just talking about the matter are necessary parts of the process. All these can and should be intentional.

* * *

In Shedd, Oregon, in 1967, the community needed a celebration of community. We decided to conduct a lawnmower derby, including a community picnic. We only put up a half-dozen posters around town and put a notice in the church newsletter. Our population in 1967 was less than 100 people in town. About 250 people showed up. The effect included the renewal of some longtime friendships. In addition, a few family farming units restructured their own covenants for labor, capital, and marketing.

* * *

The church has been involved with asking for commitment for 2,000 years. We can use this experience and our knowledge to good advantage. If we can get past the sense of being committed

46

narrowly to our own self-righteousness, we will be all right. We commit to Christ and to those whom Christ loves: all of human-kind. Then our potential community of faith becomes a reality.

*   *   *

Financial commitment campaigns for the church, or for missions, or for local needs such as a fire department or ambulance service are common in rural areas. All these bring an awareness and a habit of commitment to the fabric of the community.

Specific commitment is always a legitimate part of the life of the church. Money, time, where to purchase goods, and community services are all legitimate areas for commitment.

Brainstorm

What are your own creative thoughts on helping the community commit itself to the future?

1. What evidence have you found to support the rating you have given your own community?

2. What evidence have you found to support the rating you have given your congregation?

3. What biblical passages do you find relevant to these needs and concepts?

4. What programs might work in your church and community to enhance commitment?

5. What will your work be in this process?

6. How will you reveal these thoughts to your church and community?

Notes

Factor 5
Contribution In Community

Community Reality =   _____
Congregational Reality =   _____
Congregational Mission =   _____

> *He looked up and saw rich people putting their gifts*
> *into the treasury; he also saw a poor widow put in two*
> *small copper coins. He said, "Truly I tell you, this poor*
> *widow has put in more than all of them; for all of them*
> *have contributed out of their abundance, but she out of*
> *her poverty has put in all she had to live on."*
>
> — Luke 21:1-4

Statement Of Reality

In the contributing community, people want to give. Giving is especially important if it is to something that satisfies a need. The people accept and celebrate the contributions of all people. The people know that what they are doing is worthwhile. Systems are in place to enable every person to make their own contribution to the well-being of the community. The church is in a leadership role in the development of these systems.

Jesus' words about the scene in front of his audience were more than a call to the poor to give. He was, it appears, calling for the church to accept and recognize the gifts of even the poorest.

Big industry is a temptation for current society. We often assume only major international corporations can provide economic salvation for our communities. Fayette, Mississippi, panicked when General Motors closed a wiring harness assembly plant there. Navajos feared the prospect of a major coal company being forced out by politics or high wages. In both cases, small industry might supply jobs and benefits if it is given support in the proper areas. The church can be a major supplier of that support.

Even in slavery many have contributed to the goodness of life for the community. Many African-American and Native American slaves not only learned to read and write but taught others. Many taught their children and the children of other slaves. Some even taught their masters and the masters' children.

The migrant labor communities of the twentieth century required cooperative living. Those who could no longer work in the fields often tended and taught children. Some cared for elderly, or cared for whatever homes they could. The great civil rights struggle of the twentieth century has been to give everyone the opportunity to contribute and also the right to receive.

As pastor, I have served congregations that barred certain people from collecting the offering. Some were the wrong gender or the wrong race (whatever that means). Others were not old enough or too old. Perhaps the silliest complaint was that some did not wear the right clothes. It seems a dark suit and tie are essential parts of passing the offering plate, but I cannot even ask why. Unfortunately, most of those congregations are now out of business.

The matter of race is something we must all address. In our lifetimes we have seen this go from the all-important issues of personal quality to something quite different. Today we understand that race is nothing more than family genetic history combined with ethnicity.

Every family has a unique genetic code. This determines such things as eye color, hair, and skin, and how one's kidneys work. Combined with the ethnic accidents of history, this is our world. Some families have lived in Europe, some in Africa, and some in Asia. The problem is that folks from different families get together. They combine genes, history, creeds, and values. It is in the mixing of family genetics that biases and prejudices become rather nonsensical.

The word and the sense of race are always a matter of greed and false pride. The sense of race bars many from participating in the drive toward the vision. We can cure this division, and the church bears the primary assignment.

Questions For Evaluation

- Does our community consciously develop systems that ensure that we include everyone in its life?
- Is everyone included in the giving and receiving and speaking no matter their ethnicity, physical characteristics, age, or their own faith community?
- Do we openly seek the opinions of those presumed to be the weakest or least important of the community?
- Do we make certain the doors of opportunity and service are open to all people?

Examples

The congregation can look at its member rolls each year to discover segments of the population left out of congregational life.

* * *

The congregation can continuously look at its activities to discover if we bar some people for any reason of ability or disability, gender, education, or other factor. People with hidden or silent disabilities are particularly vulnerable to such slights. Cardiac disease is perhaps the most common in this area. Another area of vulnerability is chronic sleep deprivation. People with these disabilities often go undiagnosed throughout their lives. The church can and does frequently dismiss these individuals as simply lazy, mentally ill, or just unfaithful.

* * *

The congregation can develop and lead community events that pull people of different segments together. One of the most successful events in Winslow, Arizona, was the showing of a NASCAR race car. The congregation and the local Chevrolet dealer sponsored the event. The highlight of the day was the variety of people who climbed through the window of the car just to pretend they were driving. Elderly women, young men, Navajo, Hopi, Zuni,

51

Latino, Anglo, children, and everyone else who wished could picture themselves at Daytona Racetrack.

*   *   *

Two other events at Winslow were presentations by the United Methodist church and the presidents of the Navajo and Hopi nations. A total of about 500 people attended the two events. These led to participation by both in the annual community Thanksgiving and Christmas parade. About 10,000 witnessed this parade. The parade was the first appearance by leaders of the two nations at the same event, except in war — ever. Almost everyone credited the nations and the church with bringing about the appearances.

*   *   *

In Louisiana and many other parts of the world, Mardi Gras is a major event in local communities. The entire community lives out the sacred drama as witnessed in the faith. At Grand Marais, a community of less than 1,000 people, 20,000 showed up for the big parade. The parade is mostly high school bands, walkers, and many semi-trucks hauling people. Those on the trucks throw strings of plastic beads at the crowd. Not a bad turnout for a family show.

*   *   *

At Little Rock, Washington, we received a request from a pastor in Australia for help. He was preparing a special wedding service for his daughter, and he needed suggestions for the service.

At a Family Day worship service, we took a computer terminal into the sanctuary. During the sermon, we discussed family and marriage. While we discussed the potential service, my wife, Donella, wrote several lengthy emails to the pastor in Australia. By the end of the service, we had sent him several very strong suggestions. He immediately sent us his first responses in return.

We did, however, neglect one task. We should have sent these same emails to our own congregation! We did print them out later for everyone.

Brainstorm

What are your own creative thoughts to help everyone make their own contribution to the community?

1. What evidence have you found to support the rating you have given your own community?

2. What evidence have you found to support the rating you have given your congregation?

3. What biblical passages do you find relevant to these needs and concepts?

4. What programs might work in your church and community?

5. What will be your work in this process?

6. How will you reveal these thoughts to your church and community?

Notes

Factor 6
Continuity In Community

Community Reality =   _____
Congregational Reality =   _____
Congregational Mission =   _____

> *For I am about to create new heavens and a new earth;
> the former things shall not be remembered or come to
> mind.... No more shall there be in it an infant that lives
> but a few days, or an old person who does not live out
> a lifetime; for one who dies at a hundred years will be
> considered a youth, and one who falls short of a hundred
> will be considered accursed. They shall build houses
> and inhabit them; they shall plant vineyards and eat
> their fruit. They shall not build and another inhabit;
> they shall not plant and another eat; for like the days
> of a tree shall the days of my people be, and my chosen
> shall long enjoy the work of their hands.*
> — Isaiah 65:17, 20-22

Statement Of Reality

The community structures that work stay in place long enough to be productive. People want and need to see the results of their labors. If the community is changing groups, enough continuity is in place to see that positive values live on. Clergy and lay leadership are left in place long enough to establish programs, see results, and celebrate the community efforts.

The nation, Israel, has been a study in continuity and lack of continuity for around 4,000 years. When Abraham left the area we know as Iraq with his people, they left continuity behind. No one knows how long their ancestors had lived in that area. They settled

55

in the area with established homes, institutions, businesses, and culture. By leaving the area, they left all their community support behind. Poverty, social disruption, war, hunger, and early death were likely.

However, Israel took with them the covenant Abraham had made with Yahweh. This was the basic continuity they needed to eventually build a new society. The whole of the scriptures is the tension between continuity with the past and hopeful vision of the future. This struggle is lived out in the presence of the Lord. That presence especially was known in the covenant. This was their continuity. Without it, however, all apparently would have been lost.

Mora County, New Mexico, has been a place of refuge and restart for hundreds of years. Family after family of early Americans came into the area from Alaska, Europe, Africa, or eastern North America. They often escaped disaster from places across the nation. Eventually they left Mora to take over some better piece of land away from Mora County. Then a new nation settled in Mora to replace them. The refugees always had little in the way of cooking ability, culture, or hope. They built everything from scratch.

In Mora County, the young nations had time to put things together for themselves. They seemed to understand they were just passing through but needed to have time to build a community. The North American refugees developed their own culture and government around Mora. They rebuilt their religion to deal with the new realities of life in this inhospitable area.

The toughest part of this scenario was that each group had to start over. Each group gave up everything to rebuild.

A sure sign of a community in trouble is the transient nature of professional service in the area. Clergy, school leadership, attorneys, bank officers, and physicians stay only a short time before moving on. Sometimes, as in the case of clergy and school administrators, the community forces them to leave. For others, the decision is one's own and is often excused by a better opportunity elsewhere or something similar.

A major failing of the church is the frequency of pastoral change. In the small congregation, the pastor may initiate many good programs. The pastor carries them out almost individually;

then moves on. This leaves the congregation as weak as the day the pastor arrived. One can usually spot the weakest congregations quickly by counting the number of its pastors over the past twenty years.

My wife and I have made a lifelong pattern of accepting the task of pastoral leadership in troubled congregations. This has not been an easy pattern for service, but it has been educational.

One principle has become clear. If a congregation has problems holding on to pastoral leadership, the congregation is in trouble. The outer data is only the symptom of the reality of that congregation. Infighting within the congregation or the community may spell disaster for continuity. A self-important controlling group within the congregation may fight for control. A frequent turnover of pulpit committee leadership may be a symptom. Any problem, if carried throughout the congregation, can be destructive to the congregation, and thus to the life of the community. Frequent pastoral change is usually a prime symptom of internal trouble.

Questions For Evaluation
- Does our community have a core of professional leadership that has remained stable for many years?
- Does the core change only with honest career moves or personal needs?
- Do we have patterns of clergy leaving after a few months or a year or two?
- Do we have difficulty bringing in and keeping physicians, nurses, dentists, attorneys, school administrators, and top teachers?

Examples
(This is an example of what not to do — the pastor left almost immediately.) One congregation turned the "Pastor's Study" over to the church secretary because she needed to use the room to work up the Sunday worship bulletin. They took the key to the room away from the pastor. The pulpit committee said *he* could work from home or from the church library. She needed the study for

one hour per week because a computer was there and she needed to do the worship bulletin.

* * *

In one congregation I visited in Kansas (I forget which city), I stumbled across a special service. The congregation invited the leadership of the community to come to the church for a special service. The point of the service was to thank God for the gift of these people. All the sacred time was spent telling God what these leaders and others had done in the community. Of course, many of these leaders were included in that congregation.

Brainstorm

What are your own creative thoughts to increase community continuity?

1. What evidence have you found to support the rating you have given your own community?

2. What evidence have you found to support the rating you have given your congregation?

3. What biblical passages do you find relevant to these needs and concepts?

4. What programs might work in your church and community?

5. What will be your work in this process?

6. How will you reveal these thoughts to your church and community?

Notes

Factor 7
Collaboration In Community

Community Reality =   _____
Congregational Reality =   _____
Congregational Mission =   _____

> *Thus says King Cyrus of Persia: The Lord, the God of heaven, has given me all the kingdoms of the earth, and he has charged me to build him a house at Jerusalem in Judah. Any of those among you who are of his people — may their God be with them! — are now permitted to go up to Jerusalem in Judah, and rebuild the house of the Lord, the God of Israel — he is the God who is in Jerusalem; and let all survivors, in whatever place they reside, be assisted by the people of their place with silver and gold, with goods and with animals, besides freewill offerings for the house of their God in Jerusalem.*   — Ezra 1:2-4

Statement Of Reality

Generations of Hebrews spent centuries of slavery in the Tigris and Euphrates valleys of what is modern-day Iraq. The promised release and return to the promised land must have brought a terrible temptation to the survivors.

After the years in captivity, the people must have wanted to scramble. They probably felt compelled to run, not walk, back to the land few of them had seen. The ordinary temptation would seem to have been to ignore community and race across the desert to the Jordan River. It could have been something like the Oklahoma Land Grab or the gold rushes of the nineteenth century. It might have even approached the opening of a department store on the Friday after Thanksgiving.

The repatriates apparently came back to the promised land in some orderly manner. Their order protected their sense of community. Except for the relationships with the Samaritans, things were orderly. The returnees accused the Samaritans of collaborating with the Assyrians while their cousins were in slavery. The people apparently returned in some decent order. They re-established their communities. They rebuilt their systems of collaboration and control, their synagogues, their markets, and their city walls. They rebuilt only by taking the land and facilities back from those who had stayed.

The community works together in reliable interdependence. The community functions as a bed of multiple groups and stakeholders for the community good. Interaction among groups or individuals is supportive and effective.

Chaos in community activity will destroy the best attempts at community revitalization and recovery. In five decades of community service, I have seen many organizational disasters among well-meaning people.

Collaboration is a result of training, leadership, and commitment. It is also a result of recognizing a common calling from a common leader, Jesus of Nazareth.

The United States is an interesting experience in human activity. Although we have many differing faiths, abilities, dreams, and persuasions, we can and do work together. We are a people torn apart by civil war, yet able to recover to support civil rights. We have changed from a rural nation to an industrial nation, yet work hard to remain "small town" in spirit. Our society has chosen to defend personal freedoms. We have also become nervous when anyone uses their freedom to speak disparagingly of our system. In short, much of what keeps us together is our choice to be together. It is our common work for the good of all the world that makes us viable.

When disaster strikes, we collaborate. Military personnel, church and nonprofit volunteers, business leaders, utility workers, and many others sweating together for a common goal is our practice. Pastors shovel sand into bags held by company presidents. Muslims struggle to find and rescue Christian children caught in the aftermath of tornadoes. This collaboration is at the heart of the nature of the whole North American continent. It is also at the heart of efforts to build national and international economies around the world.

Questions For Evaluation
- Does our community support the collaborative efforts of all its groups and individuals?
- Do we work together for the good of everyone?
- As a congregation of Christ, do we invest our personal and corporate resources for the good of the community?
- Are there groups that refuse to work with other groups in the community?
- Are these isolationist groups recognized and targeted by other groups within the community?
- Do our churches, schools, and other social organizations understand collaboration within the community as an appropriate target for mission effort?

Examples
In Shady Dale, Georgia, a group of us built the first community fire truck. As part of this work we established the fire department. Junior Champion, a Primitive Baptist who drove over 100 miles each way to church on Sunday, was the leader. Junior's family and employees helped. I was the pastor of the United Methodist church. Most of the city council were Southern Baptists.

When the truck was finished, painted bright red, and outfitted with lights and siren, we drove it around the community. We gathered up volunteers for the fire department. The first man we picked up was a disabled elderly black man who lived in the town. From that point on, we had no distinction, black or white, male or female.

*   *   *

In Yachats, Oregon, the Presbyterian Church (PCUSA) has been the driving force behind a local medical clinic. Others involved were members of the local Southern Baptist church and other churches in neighboring communities. Other volunteers have come from the regional hospital, the local ambulance crew, local businesses, several local artists, and retired people.

* * *

In thousands of communities around the world, congregations gather together to celebrate the great festivals of the faith. Holy Week, Easter sunrise, Advent, and Pentecost see groups coming together for worship.

* * *

In 1998, I was serving a congregation in downtown Las Vegas. As Pentecost approached, I was a participant in an internet discussion group for clergy and laity. I entered a greeting for Pentecost from the congregation to all those who could receive it. I then suggested that those who wished should send along their own greetings. These could be in any form they wished.

Over the next several days, I received something like 200 greetings from many different faith groups and individuals. The greetings came from every continent, including Antarctica.

Others of the list followed their own path. Perhaps they ignored the messages. Perhaps they saved them. I do not know. This gathering of greetings turned out to be a treasure of ministry and understanding for our little congregation.

On Pentecost Sunday, each person who attended the small congregation received copies of several greetings. During the service I had each individual read to the congregation the greeting they held. The collaboration of the local congregation and folks on the other side of the earth was startling. It seems that instantly we had a sense of oneness with the whole church.

* * *

At Winslow, Arizona, we held the 1995 Thanksgiving morning service at the Roman Catholic church. It was my turn to speak that year. My theme was a simple one. I simply called for the community to be thankful together to God for our blessings.

As I began the message, I spoke briefly of the realities of the town. With about 12,000 people in the general community, we were in several distinct ethnic groups. Winslow has Caucasian, African-American, Mexican-American, Tex-Mex, Mexican nationals, Navajo, Hopi, Zuni, Apache, German-American, Chinese-American, Russian-American, and Irish-American, plus a few other groups that escape my memory now.

I noted that my own heritage is Welsh, Irish, Scotch, English, German, Paiute, and a few other groups mixed. I made what seemed to me an obvious remark: "I just don't know where I belong in Winslow."

It was the only time in thousands of sermons preached over a lifetime of ministry that the congregation has loudly applauded my efforts. The rest of the message focused on building acceptance and collaboration among the many ethnic groups of the community.

Brainstorm
What are your own creative thoughts toward increasing community collaboration?

1. What evidence have you found to support the rating you have given your own community for collaboration?

2. What evidence have you found to support the rating you have given your congregation for building collaboration?

3. What biblical passages do you find relevant to these needs and concepts?

4. What programs might work in your church and community?

5. What will be your work in this process?

6. How will you reveal these thoughts to your church and community?

Notes

Factor 8
Conscience In Community As A Guideline For Living

Community Reality = _____
Congregational Reality = _____
Congregational Mission = _____

> *"Come out of her [Babylon], my people, so that you do not take part in her sins, and so that you do not share in her plagues; for her sins are heaped high as heaven, and God has remembered her iniquities." ... And the merchants of the earth weep and mourn for her, since no one buys their cargo anymore, cargo of gold, silver, jewels and pearls, fine linen, purple, silk and scarlet, all kinds of scented wood, all articles of ivory, all articles of costly wood, bronze, iron, and marble, cinnamon, spice, incense, myrrh, frankincense, wine, olive oil, choice flour and wheat, cattle and sheep, horses and chariots, slaves — and human lives.... The merchants of these wares, who gained wealth from her, will stand far off, in fear of her torment, weeping and mourning aloud.* — Revelation 18:4b-5, 11-13, 15

Statement Of Reality

The ancient Hebrews seem to have struggled as much with conscience as have any people. The Lord brought the deluge to the people because of their refusal to live justly and faithfully. Noah and his family were the only survivors of the flood.

Some Hebrews accused Moses and Aaron of "lording it over" the common people among the refugees (Numbers 16). They eventually seem to have had their accusers, Korah and his people, killed for making this accusation.

Amos said other people were being destroyed for their injustices. The Hebrews would earn the same harvest.

In any election, various questions of values come forward by the voices of politicians, pundits, and voters. This is perhaps one of the finest moments of any democracy.

In every community, questions of conscience arise. The community, and especially the church, must wrestle with these. Some would argue that these questions are irrelevant to Christianity. It is my belief that these questions are at the heart of Jesus' mission.

The great witnesses to this perception are Jesus' statements in the Sermon on the Mount and especially in the Beatitudes. These statements are specific guides for the human conscience as it guides the person through life.

The community sees both the good and the evil that come from its vision, labor, and patterns. It can see what changes it must make in its value system to deal with the realities of today and tomorrow. Our community must integrate justice into the vision, the strategy, and the tactics.

Questions For Understanding
- Are we able to look at ourselves in the mirror and be certain we have lived in justice with one another?
- Have we promoted justice and lived in mutual support by the way we deal with one another in our lives?
- Do we make a strong point of doing what the Lord requires?

Questions For Evaluation
- What questions of conscience do your local media, including newspaper, radio, television, and church newsletter, cover?
- What sermons and liturgies have been built around issues of conscience in local congregations recently?
- What issues of community conscience have been topics of discussion in the community and congregation gatherings?
- What have been the outcomes of these discussions?

Examples

The struggle for civil rights has been a focus of faith community action for many centuries. The drive toward abolishing slavery has existed almost since humankind itself. The American Civil Rights Movement has depended on the church for power. Christ's church has led the movement with motivation, personnel, and struggles of conscience.

This has not been an easy matter. No particular region or faith group has had a lock on support for the Civil Rights Movement.

When Martin Luther King Jr. died in Memphis in 1968, I was serving as pastor in Pineview, Georgia. I participated in the service and the march afterward. Later I drove my Volkswagen bus west and east along the march route repeatedly. My bus and I carried mourners back to their vehicles or out to the airport. I worked at this for several hours.

On the following Sunday, the congregation at the little church I served in Pineview was most interested in that experience. I abandoned my prepared sermon that completely avoided the issue of racism and segregation. I talked, and they asked questions. They honestly wanted to know what had happened. It was probably the first time they had talked about these issues in such tones. Perhaps it was because it was in the church building. We made progress that morning, although it may have been slight.

* * *

Peace is also a matter of personal conscience and enormous consequence. If people are free to speak, someone will protest any movement toward war. That is the nature of war. It chews up everything and everyone. That leaves it squarely upon the shoulders of God's people to call things back together. We do this through study, prayer, fasting, speaking, and singing.

It seems that Jesus believed that focusing on our relationship with the creator would be the best way to live. He both implied and said explicitly that monetary wealth was not the point of life. Overall, good life would come to those who tried to make this relationship right. The missional function of spiritual activity calls us to new life. We are to find the best way to live in a world where the deity reveals the sacred presence in some way. The response to the sacred presence, if done properly, should make human life as good as it can become. That is the point of religious activity, including the work and mission of the church.

The Beatitudes are a restatement and refocus of ancient laws aimed at peace and prosperity. From some thousands of years before Christ, many had stated the secrets of the good life in legal format. Hammurabi had a lengthy detailed code nearly 2,000 years before Christ. Moses wrote down the Ten Commandments about 1,000 years later. We have records of many others.

Jesus restated the code in six or eight statements in a more positive way. He said that those who operate this way will be blessed: "Blessed is the one who hungers and thirsts for righteousness, for they will be filled."

Finally someone asked him to boil even these simple commandments down further. Jesus complied by saying, "You know the great commandment, 'You shall love the Lord your God with all your heart, with all your mind, with all your soul, with all your strength.' The second commandment is like it. 'You shall love your neighbor as yourself.' "

Brainstorm

What are your own creative thoughts toward developing a more adequate conscience?

1. What evidence have you found to support the rating you have given your own community for conscience?

2. What evidence have you found to support the rating you have given your congregation for building conscience?

3. What biblical passages do you find relevant to these needs and concepts?

4. What programs might work in your church and community?

5. What will be your work in this process?

6. How will you reveal these thoughts to your church and community?

Notes

Factor 9
Personal Mastery In Community

Community Reality = _____
Congregational Reality = _____
Congregational Mission = _____

> *"You are the light of the world. A city built on a hill cannot be hid. No one after lighting a lamp puts it under the bushel basket, but on the lampstand, and it gives light to all in the house. In the same way, let your light shine before others so that they may see your good works and give glory to your Father in heaven."*
> — Matthew 5:14-16

Statement Of Reality

The community moves toward personal mastery of the skills and character needed for community and personal life. Spiritual life, ethics, emotional well-being, social comprehension, and inner peace are realities deemed valuable to the whole person.

The *members* of the community consistently and with the support of the whole community move toward personal mastery. Their goal is to learn the skills and motivation needed for community and personal life.

King David was a master at living. He had a strength of spirituality, of war, of poetry, of love, and of many other areas. He was welcomed to the throne by many who recognized this mastery.

It turned out that David also had a mastery of introspection. At the death of his son, David was despondent, for he knew the fault was clearly his own. Much of this introspection comes out in his psalms. "Even though I walk through the darkest valley, I fear no

73

evil; for you are with me ..." (Psalm 23:4). The strength of this self-understanding braced him for the down periods of life.

Yet, it is important with David (as with all the others mentioned) that no one is master of everything. David seems to have come up short in family life. He could build a great government, write powerful poetry, and express the reality of the human situation in flowing rituals. However, David had little clue when dealing with his own family.

In Romans 12, Paul makes it clear that mastery in one area does not signify mastery in another. Yet it is good to achieve mastery in some areas and learn good skills in many others. In every community there are areas of life where someone could serve but no one has mastery. This makes it appropriate for the church or other nonprofit to develop skills among its people.

Jesus was many things to his people. Among all this he was a remarkable example of introspection. The gospels often speak of Jesus looking deep inside himself to see his own needs and directions. Even while he was with his disciples, Jesus apparently often needed to reach down deep to discover himself.

People of the renaissance emphasized the whole person. It became a style to have knowledge and expertise in many areas of life. Various academic subjects were particularly important. Astronomy, music, physics, history, dance, and many other areas were essential. Each person expected to be part of the rainbow of knowledge of the community. Even today the term "renaissance man" is one of the highest accolades toward anyone.

Personal mastery of the realities of living in community creates a comfort zone for the individual and the community around. A group of neighbors with the ability to comprehend and respond to the tougher needs of the community is a remarkable gift. It creates an amazing area of ease and personal growth.

Questions For Evaluation
- Do we encourage each other to spread ourselves to further horizons?
- Does the community take responsibility as a whole to push back these horizons?

- Is the community media engaged in broadening the scope of understanding of the citizens?
- Does each group within the community participate in this push for education?

Examples

Preparation for worship can include everyone. The worship committee and the pastor could take the time (and it is time-consuming!) to build worship from the community. They can encourage various people to dig inside themselves for the emotions, thoughts, and arts in common worship.

The primary function of the congregation is the weekly general worship service. At this time, God intends we should dredge up those experiences and thoughts inconsistent with God's vision. Then we can replace these rough spots with thoughts, emotions, and actions more in line with that vision.

In doing this we create the real possibility of and training for people becoming masters of life itself. Training for simple or complex tasks is movement toward mastery. Lighting candles, ushering, singing, speaking, and picking up used materials from the pews are important as we train toward entrepreneurship. Growth comes from mastering new experiences.

≍   *   *

Small congregations often struggle to maintain enough programs to lead a variety of people to mastery. When choosing programs, we often look at a simple target population such as the homeless, illiterate, elderly, or children. We can and should remember that the target population for all church programs includes the whole production company. The actors, performers, providers, and also those whom they serve are part of the audience.

In the church, a man who learns about cooking while feeding the homeless has received a gift toward mastery of life. A pastor who learns about autos while repairing the vehicle of an elderly person has received a gift toward mastery of life itself.

* * *

A congregation could consciously undertake, perhaps once each year, a program or event it has never done before. It might provide an Easter breakfast or perhaps a rock concert or provide a large screen television facing the street showing programs and information at all times. In Las Vegas, Nevada, some of us wanted to put up a ten-foot by ten-foot screen on the building facade. Some people objected. It seems the congregation felt it did not have the extra $100,000 to invest. Now the congregation has closed.

* * *

In Cottage Grove, Oregon, the state closed the local job service in the area with the highest unemployment rate. The congregation operated a job service for months. About three times each week we received the microfilms of jobs available around the state and nation. People looking for jobs could then read these notices at the church office. Local employers also called the church to tell of their own help needs. Several dozen people found jobs.

Brainstorm

What are your own creative thoughts toward stronger personal mastery?

1. What evidence have you found to support the rating you have given your own community for personal mastery?

2. What evidence have you found to support the rating you have given your congregation for building personal mastery?

3. What biblical passages do you find relevant to these needs and concepts?

4. What programs might work in your church and community?

5. What will be your work in this process?

6. How will you reveal these thoughts to your church and community?

Notes

Factor 10
Self-Esteem

Community Reality = _____
Congregational Reality = _____
Congregational Mission = _____

> *"Blessed are the poor in spirit, for theirs is the kingdom of heaven. Blessed are those who mourn, for they will be comforted. Blessed are the meek, for they will inherit the earth. Blessed are those who hunger and thirst for righteousness, for they will be filled. Blessed are the merciful, for they will receive mercy. Blessed are the pure in heart, for they will see God. Blessed are the peacemakers, for they will be called children of God. Blessed are those who are persecuted for righteousness' sake, for theirs is the kingdom of heaven. Blessed are you when people revile you and persecute you and utter all kinds of evil against you falsely on my account. Rejoice and be glad, for your reward is great in heaven, for in the same way they persecuted the prophets who were before you."* — Matthew 5:3-11

Statement Of Reality

Many conditions of human existence seem to destroy self-esteem. Some of these are emotional, some spiritual, and some physical, economic, or chemical. When the congregation chooses its own path, it will work to carry out that mission. The congregation will choose styles and experiences that support Christ's mission in every way. This includes building self-esteem.

A strong internal unearned value that people hold of themselves impacts the dreams and desires of the people. The people have a strong sense of their own self-esteem. The people also have a conscious drive toward building the self-esteem of others across the whole world. This drive grows from a lifetime of assurance and hope. They know they can cope with life. Yahweh and other people love them, and they know it. They know the Lord takes an active role in their support and in the bettering of their lives.

The twentieth century was a century of revolutions. Some revolutions were military, some religious, some technological, some visionary. In some, the fighters could only see a change in their visions for the possible future.

More than anything else, this vision shift for the world reflected a move toward a personal sense of worth and self-esteem. For the first time billions of people sensed that what they thought and did meant something. Before that century, the masses went through life desperately. They lived without a sense that their lives mattered to anyone, even themselves.

With the coming of massive literacy activity, democracy was finally able to gain a real foothold in the world. Even the lowest ranking citizens of the world fell heir to knowledge of international activity and its repercussions. Now we have the internet and instant polling. The citizen who chooses can literally evaluate and vote on dozens of important issues every day.

The faith revolutions of England and Europe throughout the nineteenth and twentieth centuries were major players in this change. Democracy itself enhanced and pushed this revolution ahead. Theological self-esteem and literacy technology was a direct result of the revolution. Historical insight spawns revolution.

Questions For Evaluation
- In our community, do we encourage people to participate at the strongest levels of government, industry, and community?
- Do we help our people understand the importance of their contributions to the world order?
- Does the church lead people into systems that make it possible to take personal democratic responsibility for the world?
- Do we consciously practice systems that take seriously the worth of all our community population?

Examples

In many churches across the nation, Sunday classes gather to focus on one or more of that morning's news interview shows. CBS' *Sunday Morning. Face the Nation*, and other shows make great discussion starters and decision lead-ins.

In this situation, the follow-up is critical. Comments on the issues, sent directly and quickly (either by email or snail-mail) will be very important. Often the issue will be past and forgotten if more than a few hours pass before the church speaks. A laptop computer in the meeting space can make almost instantaneous comment a real possibility.

*   *   *

We link most of our homes now by internet. We find it possible to select a topic early Sunday morning, email it to the group members, then discuss it a couple hours later in a faith group setting. Some networks make international polls every day. The class could poll its members that morning and pass along their decisions. The group could deliver the result internationally from the classroom itself. This should go far toward building self-esteem.

Any person could participate, including children, elderly, shut-ins, illiterate, disabled, non-English-speaking, and more. Large screen televisions, projection computer screens, and instant translations are possible. Our society has ways to handle all these needs. We tried this form of discussion at Mesa, Arizona, several years ago.

However, in that urban area at least one Sunday morning paper landed on the porch of almost every home represented in that class. Early Sunday morning was usually spent reading the paper rather than looking at a computer. That was a habit that was hard to break.

*   *   *

Response time immediately after the service or study group can be very helpful. At the Presbyterian church in Marcus, Washington, several attendees gathered after the service in the church basement. We talked about the sermon and the rest of the service. We gave everyone a chance to verbalize their thoughts and feelings. This helped make the work of the church more meaningful to those who did participate.

Of course, some realized that during this time they could safely disagree with the pastor. That was acceptable. The church may be the only environment where it is all right to risk growth, failure, or insight. This time was particularly challenging and rewarding to the pastor. The congregation enjoyed seeing some of the meekest in the congregation begin to blossom during these times. The blossom, however, sometimes took the form of challenging the thinking or preparation of the pastor. That was all right. In the church we have forgiveness and jubilation.

* * *

Strangely, one area of congregational life that seems to have a deep and lasting impact on individual and corporate self-esteem is the length of time the pastor serves the congregation.

If the pastor has served a long time, it seems the congregation begins to feel some success in keeping the pastor. This is sometimes true even if the pastor is not especially liked in the congregation and community.

If pastors in the congregation rotate frequently, frustration and self-doubt take up residence in the people's minds. Probably the easiest victim of this rotation is the pastor. Then, after a few pastors have come and gone quickly, the congregation has a blotched record. Potential pastors just do not choose to hear the call as easily anymore.

We should note one characteristic of congregations whose pastoral leadership rotates quickly, or congregations who cannot find pastoral leadership. We can always find a reason. This reason is rarely money. Someone will usually come forward if the other pieces of the puzzle are in place. Often a pastor will come to serve temporarily without pay.

Lack of pastoral leadership usually results from lack of clear vision and commitment within the congregation. To say it another way, if the congregation has split expectations, it is in trouble. If division exists between being pentecostal, non-pentecostal evangelical, fundamentalist, catholic, or mainstream, no pastor will last long.

A battle within such a congregation will be very destructive to everyone in the congregation and the community. I once tried to help a small congregation in just such a situation. The church was PCUSA. A minority were Free Methodists and others were Assembly of God. The secretary was demanding control as a Free Methodist. It did not and could not work.

Brainstorm
What are your own creative thoughts for building self-esteem?

1. What evidence have you found to support the rating you have given your own community for developing self-esteem?

2. What evidence have you found to support the rating you have given your congregation for building self-esteem?

3. What biblical passages do you find relevant to these needs and concepts?

4. What self-esteem programs might work in your church and community?

5. What will be your work in this process?

6. How will you reveal these thoughts to your church and community?

Notes

Factor 11
Leadership

Community Reality = _____
Congregational Reality = _____
Congregational Mission = _____

> *After the death of Moses the servant of the Lord, the*
> *Lord spoke to Joshua, son of Nun, Moses' assistant,*
> *saying, "My servant Moses is dead. Now proceed to*
> *cross the Jordan, you and all this people, into the land*
> *that I am giving to them, to the Israelites.... As I was*
> *with Moses, so I will be with you; I will not fail you or*
> *forsake you. Be strong and courageous; for you shall*
> *put this people in possession of the land that I swore to*
> *their ancestors to give them."*
>
> — Joshua 1:1-2, 5b-6

Statement Of Reality

Yahweh called Joshua in the same way Yahweh calls most of the great leaders of the world. The Lord said, in effect, "The leaders of the past are gone. Moses and Aaron have served well, but they have done their work and completed their walk. Now you have the ball. I will be beside you, as will the rest of the people of Moses. I have promised the land across the Jordan to you and your people. I will fulfill my promise through you."

Martin Luther King Jr. led some great revolutions of our world, one of which was the American Civil Rights Movement. Yet, he began as a young man with few prospects. As he grew and developed, systemic activity around him taught him the work of leadership. His family, his father's parish, his college, his seminary, the political system, black development groups, and the larger church all worked to make him the leader he became. Even Rosa Parks gave him support and motivation for his leadership by taking a forbidden seat on a city bus.

Jesus never assumed he could do all his work alone. It is clear throughout the New Testament that Jesus counted on others to continue his work. He had help leading masses of people along the path of faithfulness.

The community provides people who can make things happen. It recruits, develops, and supports them within the community. Leadership within the church is always a response to our own leader, Jesus, and discipleship to him. Leaders from the church cause things to happen in response to God's word to us. Training in leadership qualities is conscious and ongoing. Leadership is the ability to bring others along on a selected path toward the vision.

The development of leaders is not automatic. This process is a conscious act of the people. Nothing less than a full commitment to leadership development is acceptable.

In local congregations, we often repeatedly elect people to the same office because we know they can do the job. Is it not wiser to train new leaders consistently, then support them in their work? Then we can put these more experienced leaders to work in more difficult situations.

The failure of any local leader, sheriff, mayor, clerk, school administrator, or congregational leader is not just a failure of a single person. It is a failure of the community at every place along the process.

In the church, faithful people working to become leaders can practice their leadership skills. Where there are leaders, we must have followers who are in training to be leaders. In the church, our commitment is to the Lord and to each other. We will accept and support our leaders-in-training along the way.

Every office of the congregation can be a training ground for service outside the congregation. Bookkeeping, conscience building, construction, celebration, and organization can educate the community. These are just a few of the areas where the church is a prime training ground. If failure is here, at least the congregation will easily redo its structure to make failure more difficult. The church forgives mistakes, it seems, because that is what Jesus teaches.

Questions For Evaluation

- Do we consciously train future leaders? If so, what is the pattern of our training program?
- Do our churches, community nonprofits, governmental entities, and industries consciously work to develop the leaders of today and tomorrow? How?
- Is there cross-training between entities as they work to develop community leaders? How do the programs work, and who is responsible?
- Do we support those in leadership positions now? Are there benefits specifically designed for community leaders?

Examples

When a person joins a church, regardless of age, that person has the right and obligation to take full participation and service in the work of the church. Usually this includes committee membership, committee chair, lay leadership, board chair, and the like. Many rural congregations labor with only a few adults available. These same congregations may include many younger children and teens. Teens, especially, are an underused resource of the church in its mission.

Many denominations have found it necessary to specifically include children and youth in various committees and specific offices. Finance, evangelism, education, missions, and many other areas are training grounds and service opportunities.

Most congregations I have served have included at least one child or teenager on each service group. Many have found it helpful to include two of each. Usually such an arrangement offers mutual support and community acceptance for the younger set.

* * *

Leadership in various worship and discussion settings is a particularly valuable tool. Training people to lead includes training them to think through the worship service or discussion questions. This can be the most significant work of the education committee in the local church. The education committee, along with the worship committee, has an intense mission. They can prepare the training for those people who will learn to lead worship and discussion in the local church.

The worship service itself offers many opportunities for all ages to lead within the protective confines of their own congregation. Any person can write or select prayers from others' work. Any person can then speak or lead these phrases within worship. Some can prepare or speak poetry appropriate to the various portions of worship. The use of drama is healthy. Music has always been a large part of worship. Visual arts, from wall hangings to helping small children draw during service, offer another opportunity. Mission talks are appropriate. Care and repair of hymnals may be a small thing, but it is training in the details of leadership.

Many Bible readings and other liturgies satisfy specific needs for responsive use by congregations, large or small. Giving various people the opportunity and responsibility for leading these is a simple yet valuable training for leadership.

The most visible worship leadership is within the sermon or other message. Usually lay worship leadership occurs only when the pastor is absent for some reason. However, I have found that the very visible presence of the pastor is often a good help when laity delivers these messages. Limiting lay or assistant pastor preaching or speaking to occasions when the pastor is absent seems to send a message of second-rate worship to the congregation. It is therefore not good leadership training or support. Many otherwise great leaders have blown their opportunity to change the world. Leaving a legacy of prepared leadership is necessary for continuation of mission.

* * *

Many faith groups incorporate leadership training programs into their work. Conflict resolution, felt needs fulfillment, and public speaking are three of the areas usually covered in such leadership preparation. Youth groups, men's groups, women's groups, and others, are prime development arenas for leadership. The various special programs of the congregation such as Christmas and Easter programs are important here. Traditionally these times include every form of display and performance art. The congregation can readily translate these minor activities into larger leadership roles within the congregation.

*   *   *

Worship within Christianity should always be a pageant of sorts. The worship always refers to and re-enacts various events from the life of Christ. It may also include references to and acting out of other biblical and historical events.

These references and portrayals offer a myriad of opportunities for participation on various levels. Perhaps the simplest level is the infant sleeping in the manger in a Christmas pageant. Another simple level is a developmentally challenged person standing and smiling as an angel in the same pageant.

A higher level might be someone portraying the arrival of Herod's family from Edom 100 years before Jesus' birth. This could include some discussion of the Herodian attitude toward the Jewish traditions and patterns.

*   *   *

The pastor is key in developing leaders for the congregation and community. I have seen many pastors who seemed to fear that leaders might arise within the congregation. Perhaps we have a fear of competition, or a personal lack of self-esteem.

A pastor or congregation that has never sent any person into full-time Christian service may be in trouble. They should seriously question their own style and practice of leadership development.

I have had some strong participation in sending about fifteen people to full-time service. Most of them have become pastors. I count this as a mark of efficiency and a high honor.

This has been my approach. Every person is called and has the responsibility of looking at their own response to the call. Should they or should they not enter some manner of direct service?

*   *   *

The church must seriously consider the gifts and graces of every person in the congregation. As an individual, is this person appropriate for professional Christian ministry? In the United Methodist church, this action is a direct responsibility of the pastor-parish relations committee. Other groups have similar structures that must fulfill this responsibility if the church is to survive. If any person is appropriate, the congregation must approach the individual, then support that candidate in their choice. The continuing survey of the congregation for potential ministry is critical.

Brainstorm

What are your own creative thoughts for building leadership in the community?

1. What evidence have you found to support the rating you have given your own community for leadership development?

2. What evidence have you found to support the rating you have given your congregation for building leadership?

3. What biblical passages do you find relevant to these needs and concepts?

4. What programs might work in your church and community?

5. What will be your work in this process?

6. How will you reveal these thoughts to your church and community?

Notes

Factor 12
Actively Building Peace

Community Reality =   _____
Congregational Reality =   _____
Congregational Mission =   _____

> *He shall judge between many peoples, and shall*
> *arbitrate between strong nations far away; they shall*
> *beat their swords into plowshares, and their spears into*
> *pruning hooks; nation shall not lift up sword against*
> *nation, neither shall they learn war any more; but they*
> *shall all sit under their own vines and under their own*
> *fig trees, and no one shall make them afraid; for the*
> *mouth of the Lord of hosts has spoken.*
>
> — Micah 4:3-4

Statement Of Reality

Often I have seen communities with only a single missing element in the economic development package. With such a strong community, economic development should be almost automatic.

However, in several specific instances, the downward spiral of local economy continued. As I interviewed local people to uncover the issues, the major weakness became clear. We found no peace in the community. In two cases there were continuing acts of guerilla warfare or even civil war.

In one community, the open discussion of shots fired, windows broken, beatings, and threatened lynchings remind one of the situation in Iraq. The congregation there asked me not to come to that county for study. The local congregation held fear for my life. No improvement will come to that county and its economy possibly for decades to come.

93

Questions For Evaluation

- Are there signs of hostility in the local population? Racism? Religious bigotry?
- Is domestic violence a problem in your community?
- Does your congregation regularly survey local crime issues?
- What is the status of inclusiveness in your community? Are there people who feel neglected, ignored, or shut out by the community?

Examples

The congregation might hold special programs to honor various people who respond to problems in our communities: police, firefighters, utility workers, medical personnel, and so on.

* * *

If no local fire department, ambulance service, or other first responders serve the community, the congregation can be the catalyst for development of these services. The congregation might invest its own capital or money it raises in equipment for the service.

* * *

The congregation might train its own people to recognize and respond to various forms of violence in the community such as domestic violence, street violence, and school violence.

* * *

The congregation can make a variety of programs to remember community people who are part of international organizations: military, foreign service, international corporations, fraternal organizations, and the like. All these can and should be honored for making international peace a possibility and a reality.

Brainstorm

What are your own creative thoughts on the mission of peace?

1. What evidence have you found to support the rating you have given your own community for its mission of peace?

2. What evidence have you found to support the rating you have given your congregation for building its mission?

3. What biblical passages do you find relevant to these needs and concepts?

4. What programs might work in your church and community?

5. What will be your work in this process?

6. How will you reveal these thoughts to your church and community?

Notes

95

Factor 13
Streams Of Incoming Cash Flow

Community Reality = _____
Congregational Reality = _____
Congregational Mission = _____

> *Now we command you, beloved, in the name of our Lord Jesus Christ, to keep away from believers who are living in idleness and not according to the tradition that they received from us. For you yourselves know how you ought to imitate us; we were not idle when we were with you, and we did not eat anyone's bread without paying for it; but with toil and labor we worked night and day, so that we might not burden any of you. This was not because we do not have that right, but in order to give you an example to imitate. For even when we were with you, we gave you this command: Anyone unwilling to work should not eat. For we hear that some of you are living in idleness, mere busybodies, not doing any work. Now such persons we command and exhort in the Lord Jesus Christ to do their work quietly and to earn their own living. Brothers and sisters, do not be weary in doing what is right.*
> — 2 Thessalonians 3:6-13

Statement Of Reality

Cash exchange practices exist to build the money supply of the community. Adding value to the resource stream by labor or by capitalism builds the supply. All these streams are means of gathering the work and resources of multiple people into a common pool. The community (including the church) is overtly supportive of these streams and their passages within the community. The church supports people involved in developing these cash streams within the community. The commercial sector is a community resource.

The church has consistently accepted the letters to the church at Thessalonika as genuinely Paul's. The letters open with a simple statement that they come from Paul, Sylvanus, and Timothy. This is quite important but not the telling point.

The critical issue is that the letters contain thinking and verbiage that represents Paul's other known emphases. One area of Paul's concern is his insistence that we handle personal finance very carefully and openly. Each person makes his or her own contribution to society in some way.

Paul makes it plain that he works in other ways to raise money for his own expenses. The money he collects as gifts goes to other congregations who cannot support themselves. This personal responsibility, Paul knows, is a path for each of us. It is also the good path for the communities he has visited. By his own labor he helped increase their economies.

Economy grows as the value of labor, time, tools, and real property increases. Real increase comes with labor. This takes time, tools, and real property. The labor takes these supplies, adds some kind of energy, and transforms them into something more than they have been. We can adjust only the labor, the effort, and the energy. Time is what it is. It cannot change. It only flows. Energy flowing within it can change in speed and force. Real property is like time. It is what it is, but we transform our resources by our energy. Energy makes the only real change in economy.

When this energy translates into money, a serious battle can develop in the community. Do we send our money out of the community? Do we keep a larger portion of the labor/cash exchange locally? In most of the lowest-income communities of the nation, only a minimum of cash is kept within the community. Often in the lowest-income counties, more cash is sent out than is produced in the exchange. Even importing cash through outside resources such as government and church may not be enough. This practice usually moves the county deeper into poverty.

Census data shows that usually a dozen or so rural counties send out more money than the county produces. This can last only a few years before serious bankruptcy sets in. These counties typically have a per capita personal income of less than one-third the national per capita income. Sometimes they have less than one-quarter the national per capita income. Only reversing cash flow structures can effectively attack this true cycle of poverty.

A couple hundred or so counties exist wherein the money kept in the county is not enough to keep the population above the poverty level. These counties work with less than half the national per capita income.

The World Trade Center notion is that the massive majority of the world labor/money exchange travels through that complex. At one time this was a physical entity. Since September 11, 2001, the center of exchange is more a tightly woven net in south Manhattan. Once money moves into that pot, it spreads to only those agencies and people that participate in its systems. When outlying areas are not direct or powerful recipients of this amassing of wealth, poverty happens.

Questions For Evaluation
- Does our community work to bring home cash flow from other areas of the world?
- Does our community work to put its cash flow into its own income-producing labor?
- Does our church encourage the community to participate in systems that bring income into the community?
- Does the church spend its own money in our own community, or does it spend its money in other communities?
- Does our community government and industry spend money locally?
- Does the spending go to other areas where the income does not return to our community?

Examples
At Conejos, Colorado, the Roman Catholic congregation, one of the oldest in the US, rebelled at sending money to the world

church. At that time the county was one of the 25 lowest personal income counties in the nation. This act of rebellion seems to have inspired them to become more self-reliant.

This act of local ecclesiastic rebellion had a profoundly positive effect. It encouraged many local residents to do their general shopping in local stores. Previously, many were driving into Alamosa (thirty miles away) for even a loaf of bread.

*   *   *

Conejos County, Colorado, is found about thirty miles south of Alamosa. Alamosa is the shopping and service center for that part of Colorado and New Mexico. We discussed the situation with members of the congregation and the county's tourism development committee. We estimated that each trip into Alamosa for $50 of groceries cost the county $300-$400. This amount went out in lost business and additional purchases made "just because were going there anyway." Lost tax revenue, lost time, extra expenses for gasoline, and other automotive costs cost the county dearly. The area also feels the sense of lost community support and togetherness. Even the church felt that the cost of parishioners driving to Alamosa to shop was a frustration. Members drove the thirty miles, attended services, and made their contributions there.

Even the medical community of Antonito was steadily moving to Alamosa. The local college is already there. However, the lower cost of groceries in Alamosa supermarkets may save the shopper $1 or $2. Spending $400 to save $2 may not be worth the trouble.

*   *   *

At Shelley, Idaho, the congregation consciously insisted that the church purchase supplies and services locally. We began to purchase our paper, our building and maintenance supplies, and our food locally. There were several benefits.

This brought more than just business to the community. It brought the church into direct contact with local business leaders again. It raised the image of the congregation significantly. Over time, we saved money We never asked for any discount, although we frequently received discounts by local businesses. We spent far less time and money running into Idaho Falls for supplies. Calling merchandisers for supplies deliverable a week or two later was cut to a minimum by our people.

When we began the practice, we believed we could not purchase supplies locally for good prices. However, we found that local merchants could and did order supplies for us at appropriate prices. Paper and janitorial supplies were the best bargains purchased through local stores. The only supplies we had to purchase outside were denominational items and a few specialty pieces.

After a few weeks of local purchase, we began to factor in the commercial multipliers. Money spent locally typically rolls over about three times before it leaves the community. Consequently, our contribution to the local community began to seem much larger.

In addition, we discovered that several local merchants became much more receptive to support pleas for local projects. The overall financial contribution to the community was very large.

* * *

Internet shopping now enables anyone to compare prices and procedures with almost any major business around the world. This can be very good, but it can also be a danger to the local business community. It forces the local community to be very competitive in pricing and support. Few will pay extra just for the privilege of purchasing in the home community. The church must constantly keep the true cost of purchases made elsewhere in front of the people. Then they can make good choices for themselves.

Brainstorm

What are your own creative thoughts about building cash flow?

1. What evidence have you found to support the rating you have given your own community for cash stream support?

2. What evidence have you found to support the rating you have given your congregation for building cash stream support?

3. What biblical passages do you find relevant to these needs and concepts?

4. What programs might work in your church and community?

5. What will be your work in this process?

6. How will you reveal these thoughts to your church and community?

Notes

Factor 14
Not-For-Profit Groups

Community Reality =   _____
Congregational Reality =   _____
Congregational Mission =   _____

> *Beloved, do not imitate what is evil but imitate what is good. Whoever does good is from God; whoever does evil has not seen God.*   — 3 John 11

Statement Of Reality

Community groups, including the church itself, directly participate in building effective economic streams wherever appropriate. These groups work to provide a better life for the people of the community. Housing programs, media packages, and personal service programs are good mission works from any agency. In these, the labor and other support of the church add to the money provided. The congregation(s) may develop an industry, providing income for workers. It may spin these new industries off as independents, then start others. The congregation may continue to operate them. In either case, the industries become part of the total economic package of the community.

Little is spoken in the Bible of the distinction between profit and nonprofit enterprises. The work of the temple organization covered the whole of the nation geographically and socially. Otherwise, the Bible speaks little of nonprofit work.

Faithful people of many varying communities have developed not-for-profit schemes that have delivered great good to the world. Evidence says that faithfulness helps. It leads to the kind of attitude and organization that results in missional nonprofit entities.

A long history exists of faith communities taking active roles in developing both social service streams and for-profit industries. Most American faith groups have investments in industry in some form. Sometimes these investments maintain pension and insurance programs. At other times these holdings cover mission efforts.

Others have been more direct. Many have established housing projects, treatment centers, craft projects, and even direct for-profit industries. These industries are usually spun off or sold. Their major importance, though, is as seed for additional labor projects in the community. The work of organizing these industries is a part of the mission of the church. The church has money, organization, education, systems, prestige, and marketing skills that can be useful in industry.

Questions For Evaluation
• Do churches or any other nonprofit groups continually search for ways to build the economy?
• What church systems add to the economy of the local community?
• Is the church a drain on community finances or a benefit to these finances?

Examples
In many areas of eastern Kentucky and Tennessee, the Red Bird Mission of the United Methodist church operates economic support programs. Some of these are craft-oriented. Others work with donated surplus items. The programs also include medical care centers and schools. Many of those involved in these programs have a significant income and hope for the future because of the organization.

* * *

The United Methodist Committee on Relief (UMCOR) operates a sorting and shipping depot in Baldwin, Louisiana. From that facility, UMCOR sends disaster relief supplies all around the world.

The worst human disasters receive these supplies. The Sager-Brown facility sits in the heart of the hurricane belt, one of the worst disaster-prone areas known. Sager-Brown employees several people to manage and support the work.

In addition, thousands of people each year come to volunteer their time and labor to make the program feasible. These volunteers repair local homes and businesses damaged by poverty, hurricane, rain, or misuse. Without this supply of free labor, the program could not operate.

Brainstorm

What are your own creative thoughts toward helping the development of nonprofit groups?

1. What evidence have you found to support the rating you have given your own community for nonprofit service groups?

2. What evidence have you found to support the rating you have given your congregation for building nonprofit service groups?

3. What biblical passages do you find relevant to these needs and concepts?

4. What programs might work in your church and community?

5. What will be your work in this process?

6. How will you reveal these thoughts to your church and community?

Notes

Factor 15
Celebration!

Community Reality =   _____
Congregational Reality =   _____
Congregational Mission =   _____

> *O give thanks to the Lord, for he is good, for his steadfast*
> *love endures forever. O give thanks to the God of gods,*
> *for his steadfast love endures forever. O give thanks to*
> *the Lord of lords, for his steadfast love endures forever.*
> — Psalm 136:1-3

As we look at the needs of the community in economic devel-opment, the final field stands out. It is an area where religious groups, local or world, have excelled since human intelligence began to develop. Sometimes the efforts have been stuttering, and sometimes the efforts have been nothing short of spectacular. That final need, often falling short in economically deprived communi-ties, is ... celebration!

Statement Of Reality

A magnificent accounting and example of biblical-era pageantry is found in Psalm 136. Psalm 136 speaks of the whole history of Yahweh's involvement in human life. God's action, humankind's response, and then God's next action/response comes to the front of community thought. Each of these is presented in a style that makes it easily understood. This is key. If the people understand a notion, the congregation will remember and repeat the story for centuries. A shout of joy from the congregation follows each note of remembering from the congregation. This practice serves a double purpose

107

When we remember the past, we have a reminder that things have happened this way. It is also both a sobering and hopeful note. The future is likely to look the same way if the circumstances are set up in the same way. The reason people can be confident that history will come out that way again is because history depends not on man's action alone, but on God's response to mankind's action. When humans foul things up, God redeems the situation.

This pattern of history is, first, a call to judgment. We dare not expect relief if we violate God's vision. If we steal or enslave, we face a consequence within our relationship with God.

Second, the pattern is a call to hope. We may honestly expect miracles when we try to fit our lives into God's vision for us. If we struggle for peace, we can assume God will choose to work with us.

The shout of joy is a cry of thanksgiving and a theological statement. It says that "steadfast love" (*hesed*) is within the very being of the creator. God will respond to any activity by humanity with God's own steadfast love. *Hesed* can be trusted because God is God.

This cry is also a call to God's people to share in the work of ongoing creation. God makes us in the image of God, but not the reality of a god. Christ invites us to activate this steadfast love in our own lives, just as steadfast love is active in God's existence. We create as we love. Steadfast love may or may not be an option for God. I do not know. I do know we are not perfect. We can, however, begin our steadfast love by choice. We must be born again.

These words, shouts, and songs do bring smiles to the people. The people gather together with joy to sing and praise the Lord for the goodness of the Lord. By their shouts of *hesed*, they also announce their willingness to accept and emulate this steadfast love in their own lives.

In Celebration

- Every aspect of community life, positive and negative, rises up in remembering, reenacting, and feeling good.

- The community excitedly tells its own story.
- The community honestly presents the human situation to itself and to God. This is a sacrifice and thanksgiving to God. The pageant and party are well formed and intentional consequences of community action.
- Pageants, festivities, and community spiritual life experiences dealing with past and future history are commonplace and anticipated, especially in the church.

Most world communities understand well the need for celebration. County fairs, picnics, and festivals of every kind dot the world landscape. Sometimes it seems that we have little to celebrate but something can always be found.

The list of celebratory causes is endless. Sometimes it is a specifically religious matter, sometimes not. The succession of a new pope, or the birthday of Aunt Maude over in Pine Hollow qualifies nicely. Naming a new pastor to Liberty Church with its seven members is a huge event. The inauguration of a second-term president of the United States is a great opportunity for celebration. All these celebrations recall the nature of God and humanity.

We even deal with death in our celebrations. Our funerals and memorial services are exciting times for us. In them we raise our shouts of thanksgiving for God's steadfast love and our responses.

I have led several hundred memorial services over the past forty years. Perhaps the one I remember most is the last I led as pastor of a Presbyterian congregation in Stapleton, Nebraska.

An infant died of massive birth defects within a few days of birth. As I talked with the family, I slowly became aware of what I must say at the service in the church. I also was aware of what I should have said at every other celebration at the end of a life.

The church was full for that little child and the family. We read several pieces of scripture, had a few songs, and heard some poetry. Then it was my turn to put into simple, concrete words the community cry of celebration, both sadness and joy.

I began by talking about the details of the life. The family, the pregnancy with its hopes and expectations: birth, shattered dreams, hospitalization, death.

Then I talked about Jesus. The family, the pregnancy with its hopes and expectations: the birth, flight to Egypt, growing up, his death, his resurrection.

Next came two simple thoughts. First, that everything of Jesus' life can and will happen to us, if we accept it. This includes the resurrection.

Second, that every life is complete, no matter how long it lasts. Jesus' life lasted only about thirty years. His life was complete because he loved and was loved. The gospels are the love story between Jesus and the people around him. What other factors could be important enough to say that, if Jesus lacked them, his life was incomplete?

The baby of this family had a complete life. It was complete because the baby loved and was loved. This service was the formal record of that love within the community. What other factors could be important enough to say that, if this child lacked them, his life was incomplete?

The church, by its own nature, must train the community in the art and practice of celebration. When a congregation holds a Thanksgiving dinner, that is, in part, a way of training the community to celebrate. Therefore, it must be done systematically and carefully, with due planning and promotion.

Questions For Evaluation
- Does our community celebrate itself?
- Does the church work to develop its own life and the life of the community in a way that promotes a sense of celebration?
- Is every group within the community, including churches, industries, schools, fraternal groups, and recreational activities, included in support of community celebrations?
- Do we feel good about being whose we are?

Examples
In 1966 in Shedd, Oregon, we knew we needed a celebration. Shedd was faltering. Stores and schools were closing. We feared the church would be next, so the church began the first annual

international lawnmower racing championships. An appropriate picnic went along with the races, and we had a great day.

*   *   *

Worship is always a celebration of something. Christian worship can and should be a celebration of life itself. If life is a gift from the creator, our celebration becomes a way of saying "Thanks!" No matter the time, place, circumstance, or faith group, Christians must always celebrate Jesus' life and ministry. It is the nature of the faith.

We build our theology around a creator who chooses to take an active, benevolent role in our lives. Our faith is best defined as a three-way relationship. Picture a triangle. The three points represent God, the rest of humanity, and your own self. The lines between the points represent the relationships among the three parties involved. This is the basic structure of faith.

The three-way relationships between God, other people, and ourselves will be quite similar. Our way of relating to God is the way we will also relate to other people. Our relationship with others will be one of the building blocks of their relationship with God.

In the middle of this stands the church. The role of the church is threefold, as well. That role is, first, to model God's vision of the relationships between God and humanity. Second, it is to move all parties to adopt that vision for their own lives. Third, the role of the church is to help us release the thankful celebrative energy within us and within God. In short, the church helps us continually build and rebuild our faith.

We can celebrate this. We can celebrate (shout about, sing about, pray for and about, speak poetry about, and more) almost anything. We can celebrate the end of war, marriage, or elephants. Almost every day of the year is an anniversary in some way. We can celebrate famine relief, crops, fishing, or that it is Sunday or Tuesday!

We can celebrate the work of the disciples, or the first people living in our area thousands of years ago. We can celebrate the

111

invention of irrigation systems, horseradish, the softness of baby's skin, forgiveness, those who build schools, and our community leaders. We can celebrate those whose service can only be to love and to receive God's love and our love.

Our causes for celebration include the birth, life, death, and resurrection of Jesus of Nazareth. The congregation of the local church is a cause for celebration. I often tell congregations that I really don't understand why they have come on that day. It must have been God's choice, somehow. The serendipity of me having something to say, the congregation coming at that specific time, and our sharing of songs and celebrations are all God's design. Let's celebrate it together.

*   *   *

Marriage is also a celebration of relationships of love. Weddings, funerals, and baptisms can be beautiful celebrations of human and divine relationships. An entire congregation can struggle with the meaning and value of any of these. It can also reveal its own lack of relational depth.

One congregation told me I was not to accept anymore weddings. "It makes us look like a wedding chapel." Gosh, I didn't know that celebrating a marriage was a bad thing for Christians. At my own expense, I made pictures of many weddings I performed at that church and I hung them in a hallway. One couple or another came back almost every week to look at their picture and mentally renew their vows. When we left there, the congregation took down those pictures and sent them to me. They did not want to burn them.

Brainstorm

What are your own creative thoughts toward building celebration patterns in your community?

1. What evidence have you found to support the rating you have given your own community for community celebration?

2. What evidence have you found to support the rating you have given your congregation for building congregational celebration?

3. What biblical passages do you find relevant to these needs and concepts?

4. What celebrations might work in your church and community?

5. What will be your work in these processes?

6. How will you reveal these thoughts to your church and community?

Notes

Appendix

Individual Rating Sheet For The Church And The Financial Well-Being Of The Local Community

A Church That Matters

Every caring Christian knows the critical value of personal income within the community. It is incredibly important to the well-being of the local church. The church lives on the contributions of its members and non-member supporters. It can and should focus part of its mission work on factors that affect the economic life of the local community. By comprehending the thinking of Jesus, the church will search for ways to live out Jesus' mission. It will support individuals, families, and communities in all portions of their personal lives, including economic development.

Getting Started In Our Own Community

In economic development we find a wide-open field for the mission of Christ. The church and other charitable nonprofits have the tools and the personnel to step in and make a huge difference. People plainly want support from Christ in their daily lives. This support comes first and best from local congregations.

Defining A Mission Of Economic Development For Christian Congregations And Other Nonprofits

In the first space of each factor in the following form, grade your community. On a scale of zero to ten (0-10), with ten being high, rate the general level of each factor in your community. Take into account all you know about your community, its history, and its people. Be as critical and as complete as you wish. No one will call you wrong for your judgment. It is very personal.

In the second space of each factor, give your congregation a reality mark (0-10) for itself. Again, lift up as much as you wish about your congregation and your denomination. Consider your administration, the gatherings, mission programs and giving, worship, sacramental style, and other relevant areas.

In the third space of each factor, use the same scale for the strength and efficacy of the congregational commitment to build healthy factors in your community. Ask yourself what would Jesus say or do when faced with the needs of the people in your community today. These needs will be the same for all people whether in the US or other nations. Perhaps we should ask what Jesus did, according to the gospels. Then we could judge our own efforts accordingly.

The Reality Of Our Community

A worksheet is provided for each factor to aid the study of our community and congregation. Each person should complete his or her own worksheets. This can be done in a large group meeting or while working as individuals or small groups.

Notes

Factor 1
The Sense Of Creation

Community Reality =   _____
Congregational Reality =   _____
Congregational Mission =   _____

The community senses creation as a personal gift from God. It therefore needs to command as much respect, gratitude, concern, and understanding as we can muster. God creates the world and humankind, then comes to us bearing gifts. Matters of ecology and resources are of intense concern for all.

Notes

Factor 2
Vision In Community

Community Reality =   _____
Congregational Reality =   _____
Congregational Mission =   _____

Christ has shared with us the sacred vision for this world and the next. He has told us what God wants, expects, and what God brings into reality. It is also what God knows to be in our best interest. God's vision for us is that we should have the best possible life. We may buy into that vision for each other and ourselves.

Notes

Factor 3
Capability In Community

Community Reality = _____
Congregational Reality = _____
Congregational Mission = _____

Community residents have the skills, knowledge, resources, and personal qualities to renew themselves and reinvent their future. They learn collectively and individually. Learning has a high priority as a community activity. Basic skills of living in community (reading, math, listening, and so on) are present in most of the population.

Notes

Factor 4
Commitment In Community

Community Reality = _____
Congregational Reality = _____
Congregational Mission = _____

People are actively creating something they value together. Current common commitments to the community vision guide personal and corporate life. Strong processes to develop updated commitments to each other and to the future ensure a constantly renewed vision. The church has an active leadership role developing and supporting these commitments.

Notes

Factor 5
Contribution in Community

Community Reality = _____
Congregational Reality = _____
Congregational Mission = _____

People want to give, especially if it is to something they feel is worthwhile. The community accepts and celebrates the contributions of all people. The people want to know that what they are doing is worthwhile. Systems are in place to enable every person to make their own contribution to the well-being of the community. Christ's church is in a leadership role in the development of these systems.

Notes

Factor 6
Continuity In Community

Community Reality =   _____
Congregational Reality =   _____
Congregational Mission =   _____

    The community structures that work stay in place long enough to be productive. People want and need to see the results of their labor. If the community is changing groups (redeveloping), we have enough continuity in place to support productive values and people. Clergy and lay leadership needs to be left in place long enough to establish programs, see results, and sense support for their efforts.

Notes

Factor 7
Collaboration In Community

Community Reality =   _____
Congregational Reality =   _____
Congregational Mission =   _____

The community works together in reliable interdependence. The community functions as a web of families acting toward the good of everyone. Interaction among groups or individuals is supportive, effective, and honored.

Notes

Factor 8
Conscience In Community As A Guideline For Living

Community Reality = _____
Congregational Reality = _____
Congregational Mission = _____

The community can see the good and the evil that comes from its vision, its labor, and its patterns. It can see needed changes for its value system. These allow the community to deal rightly with the realities of today and tomorrow. Community conscience integrates justice into the vision, the strategy, and the tactics.

Notes

Factor 9
Personal Mastery In Community

Community Reality = _____
Congregational Reality = _____
Congregational Mission = _____

Individuals consistently move toward the quality of skills needed for community and personal life. Spiritual life, ethics, emotional well-being, social comfort, and inner peace are critical to the whole person.

King David was considered a master at living. He had a strength of spirituality, of war, of poetry, of love, and of many other areas. He was welcomed to the throne by many who recognized this mastery. Are the people of the community as prepared as David was?

Notes

Factor 10
Self-Esteem

Community Reality = _____
Congregational Reality = _____
Congregational Mission = _____

The people hold a strong, unearned internal view of themselves. The community population builds its self-esteem from a lifetime of assurance knowing they can cope with life. People know that the Lord and other humans love them. They know the Lord takes an active role in their support and in the bettering of their lives. The people see themselves as being of unlimited worth in the eyes of their creator and their neighbors.

Notes

Factor 11
Leadership

Community Reality =   _____
Congregational Reality =   _____
Congregational Mission =   _____

The community recruits, develops, and supports people who can make things happen within the community. Leadership within the church is always a response to our own leader, Jesus, and discipleship to him. Leaders from the church cause things to happen in response to God's word. Training in leadership skills is conscious and ongoing. Leadership is the ability to bring others along on a selected path toward the vision.

Notes

Factor 12
Actively Building Peace

Community Reality = _____
Congregational Reality = _____
Congregational Mission = _____

The gentle mixing of the aims and values of many is a precious style within the community. Compassion is an expected attribute of leadership. The community seeks peace both as value and as style within group and individual relationships.

Notes

Factor 13
Streams Of Incoming Cash Flow

Community Reality =   _____
Congregational Reality =   _____
Congregational Mission =   _____

The resources of labor and capitalism add value to the stream of cash flow. Our community (including the church) is overtly supportive of these streams and their passages within the community. The church supports people working to develop these cash streams within the community. The commercial community functions as a precious resource.

Notes

Factor 14
Not-For-Profit Groups

Community Reality =   _____
Congregational Reality =   _____
Congregational Mission =   _____

Community groups, including the church itself, directly build effective economic streams wherever appropriate. These groups work to fulfill the vision for the community. This includes efforts such as housing programs, media packages, and personal service programs. Results of these efforts add to the work of other profit and nonprofit groups and individuals. The congregation(s) may develop industries that provide income for workers. These industries may be spun off and others developed, then others started. These become part of the total economic package of the community.

Notes

Factor 15
Celebration!

Community Reality =   _____
Congregational Reality =   _____
Congregational Mission =   _____

Every aspect of community life, positive and negative, occasionally erupts in remembering, reenacting, and feeling good. The community excitedly tells its own story. The community honestly presents the human situation to itself and to God. Public worship is a sacrifice and thanksgiving to God. The pageant and party are well formed and are intentional consequences of community action. Pageants, festivities, and community spiritual life experiences deal with past and future history. These are commonplace and anticipated, especially in the church.

Notes

Recap: Individual Scores

Add your total scores for each area together. Then divide by 150 for the total possible individual score.

Total Community Reality =
_____ ÷ 150 = _____ (Overall Net Score)
This score reflects your assessment of the preparedness of your community for economic development.

Total Congregational Reality =
_____ ÷ 150 = _____ (Overall Net Score)
This score reflects your own individual assessment of the preparedness of your congregation for local economic mission work.

Total Congregational Mission =
_____ ÷ 150 = _____ (Overall Net Score)
This score reflects your own individual assessment of the will of your congregation to live out Christ's mission in your own community.

Recap: Group Scores

Add all scores from the study group together. Divide by the number of participants, then by 150 for the total possible individual score.

Total Community Reality =

_____ ÷ _____ ÷ 150 = _____ (Overall Net Score)

This score reflects your group assessment of the preparedness of your community for economic development in the factors listed here.

Total Congregational Reality =

_____ ÷ _____ ÷ 150 = _____ (Overall Net Score)

This score reflects your group assessment of the preparedness of your congregation for local economic mission work.

Total Congregational Mission =

_____ ÷ _____ ÷ 150 = _____ (Overall Net Score)

This score reflects your group assessment of the will of your congregation to live out Christ's mission in your own community.

This exercise should help the congregation understand and accept a local mission role. This role will affect the community by bringing the word of Christ to bear on local life.

About The Author

Karl Evans grew up in a Christian home near Fruitland, Idaho, on a family farm located in a new farming area. This experience shaped his thinking on economic development.

As a United Methodist pastor in several states, he tried to listen. He heard hundreds of people pour out their personal stories of life. All these stories laid the groundwork for this writing.

Doctor Evans holds a B.A. from Williamette University (Religion and Psychology), an M.Div. from Emory University (Pastoral Ministry), and a D.Min. from Drew University (Storytelling in Ministry). In addition, he attended the University of Puget Sound and Grays Harbor College.

Karl has served pastorates in Washington, Oregon, Idaho, Georgia, Arizona, and Nevada. His denominational service has included United Methodist, Presbyterian Church in the USA, and the Evangelical Lutheran Church in America. Karl has also served with the United Methodist General Board of Global Ministries as staff and contracted consultant. His areas of service include congregational development and poverty research. Karl also worked with the Wesley Community Center in Phoenix, Arizona.

Karl and his wife, Donella, have four children, ten grandchildren, and five great-grandchildren.

www.ingramcontent.com/pod-product-compliance
Lightning Source LLC
Chambersburg PA
CBHW060906280326
41934CB00007B/1208